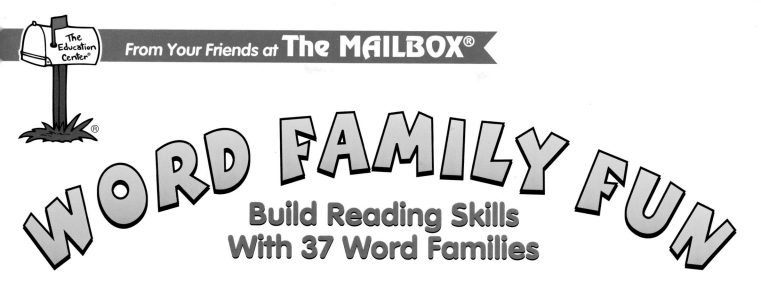

From Your Friends at The MAILBOX®

WORD FAMILY FUN

Build Reading Skills With 37 Word Families

Grades 1–2

Written by:
Mary Lester, Laura Mihalenko, Linda Morgason

Edited by:
Amy Erickson, Hope H. Taylor

Illustrated by:
Cathy Spangler Bruce, Pam Crane, Theresa Lewis Goode, Clevell Harris,
Sheila Krill, Kimberly Richard, Greg D. Rieves, Rebecca Saunders
Barry Slate, Donna K. Teal

Cover designed by:
Kimberly Richard

www.themailbox.com

©2000 by THE EDUCATION CENTER, INC.
All rights reserved.
ISBN #1-56234-396-3

Manufactured in the United States
10 9 8 7 6 5 4 3 2 1

Table of Contents

About This Book

Beginning literacy skills are all in the family with this handy resource! Featuring 37 common word families, this book is packed with creative activities designed to help students feel right at home with reading and writing.

Why Study Word Families?

Skilled readers recognize patterns in words rather than sound words out, letter by letter. Word families, also known as phonograms, rimes, or chunks, are letter patterns that are more stable than individual vowel sounds. Readers can use word families to decode by analogy—use what they know about one word to decode another. If a reader knows the word *tack,* for example, it's likely that he will be able to read other *-ack* words, such as *snack* and *jacket.* Youngsters often find it easier to use a word family to decode a word than to break it into syllables or individual letter sounds.

The word families presented in this book can be used to make about 500 primary words and many multisyllable words. A multisyllable word might have more than one word family, and the rimes may be found anywhere in the word (for ease in reading, this book indicates each word family with one hyphen preceding it, rather than one on either side). With sharp word family skills and context clues, young readers can decode many multisyllable words. There's no doubt about it, word family skills are powerful tools for building literacy!

How Does This Book Reinforce Word Family Skills?

A two-page unit is provided for each of the 37 word families. Each unit includes

- **Word List:** Make a copy for each student to take home for additional reading practice or to cut out and glue onto a writing folder for a convenient reference.

- **Set the Foundation:** An introductory activity.

- **Build Skills:** An idea to develop students' proficiency with the word family.

- **Add Extensions:** An activity or list of literature to extend students' learning. After sharing the literature for enjoyment, use it for activities such as word family hunts.

- **Reproducible:** Patterns or a skill sheet.

The book also includes other practical ideas and reproducibles, such as activities that can be used with any word family and mixed practice skill sheets. An informal assessment tool (see page 78 for instructions) provides a simple way to determine a student's ability to decode words with rimes of increasing difficulty.

Note: Every title listed was in print at the time of this book's publication. If you have difficulty locating any of the featured titles, check with your media specialist.

Should the Units Be Used in Order?

Not necessarily. The units are arranged in alphabetical order for easy reference but may be used in any order. Short-vowel word families are not necessarily easier for students than long-vowel word families. Context and many other factors influence youngsters' performance.

-ack

back

black

cracker

Jack

jacket

packed

rack

sack

snack

stacking

tack

track

SET THE FOUNDATION

What better way to introduce -ack words than with the well-known (and silly) character, Miss Mary Mack? To prepare, write "-ack" on a white card and glue it near the top of a poster-sized piece of black bulletin board paper. Then put the poster aside, along with a supply of white cards.

To begin, read aloud *Miss Mary Mack: A Hand-Clapping Rhyme* by Mary Ann Hoberman (Little, Brown and Company; 1998). Then write "Mack," "black," and "back" on the board. Ask youngsters what they notice about these words. Lead them to conclude that each word contains the -ack word family.

Next, display the poster within easy student reach. Challenge youngsters to brainstorm -ack words. With students' help, write each word on a card and glue it to the poster. Then, for each word, ask a different student to underline the featured word family with a red marker. For added fun, pair students and invite them to try the traditional Miss Mary Mack rhyme with a simple hand-clapping pattern. Now that's a crackerjack idea!

BUILD SKILLS

Here's a booklet project that's packed with word family practice! For each student, make one copy of the backpack pattern, one copy of the cover pattern, and four copies of the page pattern (page 5). Distribute the copies. Read the text on the backpack aloud with students. Then have each youngster make a booklet packed with -ack words.

To make his booklet, the student writes and illustrates a different -ack word on his backpack and on each of his pages. (Be sure that he orients each page so that the line is at the bottom.) The youngster writes his name on the cover. Then he colors the backpack and the cover, being careful to leave the words visible. The youngster cuts out the backpack, cover, and pages. He stacks the pages, places the cover atop them, and then staples the entire stack to his backpack. Invite each student to read the cover text and booklet pages to a classmate before taking his work home to share with his parents.

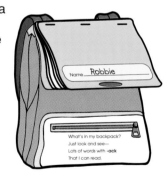

ADD EXTENSIONS

Reinforce the -ack word family with these great titles!
This Is The House Jack Built by Pam Adams (Child's Play [International] Ltd, 1995)
Come Back, Jack! by Catherine Anholt and Laurence Anholt (Candlewick Press, 1996)
Lazy Jack by Vivian French (Candlewick Press, 1997)

Cover Pattern

Name

Page Pattern

Backpack Pattern

What's in my backpack?
Just look and see—
Lots of words with **-ack**
That I can read.

Note to the teacher: Use with "Build Skills" on page 4.

-ail

fail

hail

jail

mail

mailbox

nail

pail

railing

sail

snail

tail

trail

SET THE FOUNDATION

Shed light on the -ail word family with these unique letter manipulatives! To prepare, cut one blank transparency sheet into 2" x 2³/₄" pieces. Use an over-head marker to write "ail" on one piece. On the remaining pieces, use different-colored markers to write the following (note that the last three are word endings): *b, f, h, j, m, n, p, r, s, t, tr, ed, ing, s.*

To begin, read aloud *Hooray for Snail!* by John Stadler (HarperTrophy, 1985), an easy-to-read book about a baseball-playing snail. Then, with students' help, use the prepared transparency letters to form *snail* on an overhead projector. Ask a student volunteer to remove a letter to make *nail.* Invite different students to form other -ail words in a similar manner. On a sheet of paper, have each young-ster write an original sentence about Snail with one or more -ail words and then illustrate his work.

BUILD SKILLS

It's time to sort the mail! Give each student a copy of page 7. Have each youngster color the front of the mailbox, cut out the mailbox along the bold line, and cut the dotted line to make an opening. Instruct him to fold the mailbox on the fine line, staple it where indicated, and then cut out the envelopes.

To sort his mail, the youngster reads each envelope. If the word has the -ail word family, he writes it on the back of his mailbox. If it does not, he puts the envelope aside to discard later. Then the student places all of his -ail word envelopes in the mailbox slot. After verifying his work, encourage each youngster to take his mail home to share with his family. Now that's a word family activity that really delivers!

ADD EXTENSIONS

This fast-paced class activity is sure to put students hot on the trail of -ail words! For each student, write these sentences on a card and complete them with two different -ail words: "I have the word _____. Who has the word _____?" Prepare each card so that the second sentence on one card is answered by the first sentence on another card (see the illustration). Then randomly distribute the cards. Ask a student volunteer to read her card aloud. Have the classmate who has the response read her own card aloud. Continue in a like manner until all of the stu-dents have read their cards.

I have the
word <u>snail</u>.

Who has the
word <u>tail</u>?

I have the
word <u>tail</u>.

Who has the
word <u>mail</u>?

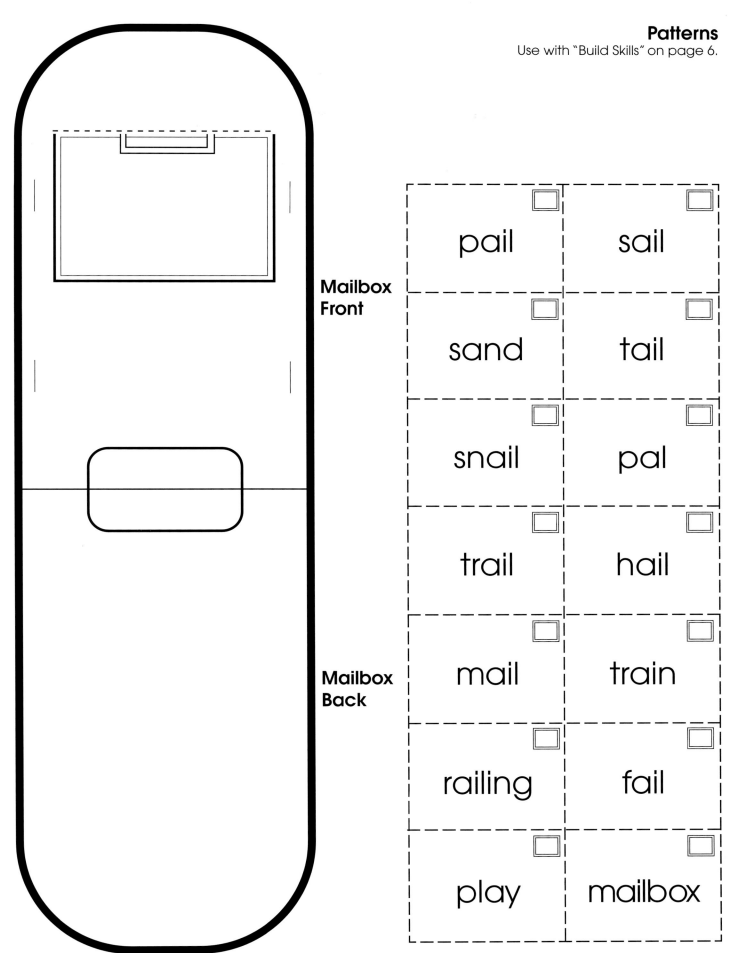

Mailbox Front

Mailbox Back

pail	sail
sand	tail
snail	pal
trail	hail
mail	train
railing	fail
play	mailbox

-ain

brain

chain

drain

gain

grain

main

pain

plain

rain

raincoat

stain

train

SET THE FOUNDATION

What's in the forecast? Plenty of -ain word fun! Show students the cover of Rain by Robert Kalan (Mulberry Books, 1991). Read the title; then ask youngsters to tell what they notice about the illustration. Lead them to conclude that the word rain is shown repeatedly to resemble actual rain. As you read the book, encourage students to watch for similar types of word-created illustrations. Then have students use a simple variation of this illustration technique to create a rainy day mural.

To make the mural, brainstorm -ain words. Then give each youngster a light blue raindrop cutout. Have him write an -ain word of his choice on the cutout. Display a mural-sized piece of white bulletin board paper, and divide students into small groups. Have each group, in turn, glue its raindrops on the paper and then add details with crayons to incorporate the raindrops into a scene. Then display the mural for all to admire. It looks like rain!

BUILD SKILLS

With this reproducible activity, students are sure to have -ain words on the brain! Give each student a copy of page 9. Have each student write and illustrate three or four -ain words between the top dotted line and the solid line. Then ask her to color the illustration and face as desired, being careful to leave the words visible. Instruct each youngster to fold her paper on the dotted lines as shown. Then pair students and have each youngster share her work with her partner. Now that's a brainy word family idea!

ADD EXTENSIONS

Watch word family skills grow with this -ain word display! Give each student five to eight 1½" x 10" strips of light-colored construction paper. The youngster writes a different -ain word on each strip and then makes a chain by gluing his strips together with the words facing out. He uses the words to write a story on provided paper; then he illustrates his work. Post each youngster's story on a bulletin board titled "Chains of Events." Display his chain with the story or have students link their chains together to make one long class chain; then staple it along the edges of the board.

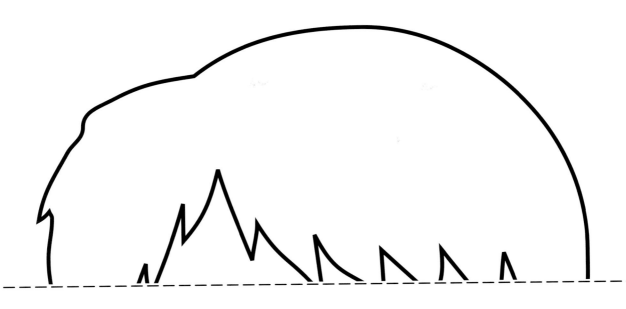

Note to the teacher: Use with "Build Skills" on page 8.

-ake

bake

brake

cake

cupcake

fake

flake

lake

make

rake

shake

take

wake

SET THE FOUNDATION

In *Pancakes, Pancakes!* by Eric Carle (Aladdin Paperbacks, 1998), Jack decides that making pancakes takes a lot of work. But with this appetizing idea, your students can whip up a batch of word pancakes in a snap! After reading the story aloud, use manipulative letters to spell *pancake*. Read the word with students, drawing their attention to the *-ake* word family. Then ask volunteers to remove or add letters to form other *-ake* words.

Next, divide students into small groups. Give each group a set of manipulative letters, crayons, scissors, one sheet of gray construction paper, and several sheets of manila paper. Have the group form an *-ake* word with its letters, make a pancake-shaped cutout from the manila paper, and then copy the word onto the cutout. After every group has prepared several pancakes, have one student in each group make a skillet-shaped cutout from gray paper. Display each group's pancakes and skillet on a board titled "Flipping Over -ake Words!"

BUILD SKILLS

Celebrate *-ake* words with this mouthwatering activity! Give each student a copy of page 11. To decorate her cake, the student writes *-ake* words on the frosting. Then she writes a sentence on the lines, using one or more of the words. The youngster outlines her cake and frosting with crayons, cuts out the cake, and then glues on construction paper candles for a festive touch. To recognize your young chefs' hard work, top off the activity by serving a yummy treat of cupcakes. Reading has never tasted so good!

ADD EXTENSIONS

Shake out *-ake* words (and wiggles!) with this lively listening activity. Prepare a list of *-ake* words that is interspersed with several words that do not have this word family. Ask each student to stand by his chair. Explain that you will read some words aloud. If a word has the *-ake* word family, each student should shake his arms and hands. If a word does not have the word family, he should shake his head no. Read aloud the first word. Allow time for students to respond; then call on a youngster who responded correctly. Ask him to repeat the word and state whether or not it has the *-ake* word family. Continue with the remaining words in a like manner.

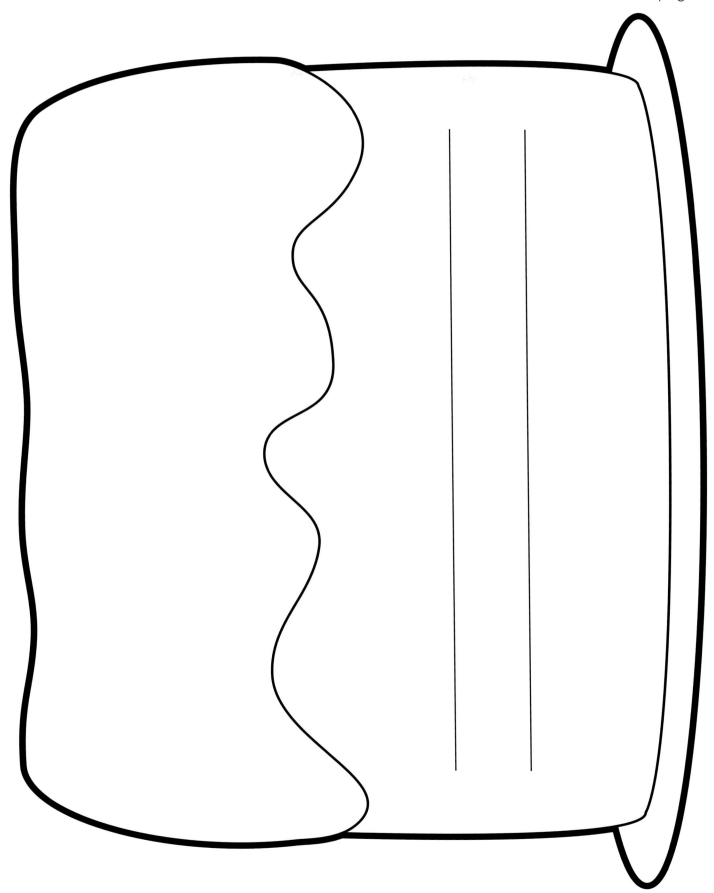

-ale

bale

dale

female

gale

inhale

male

pale

sale

scale

stale

tale

whale

SET THE FOUNDATION

Words! Words for sale! Cash in on lots of learning fun with -ale words! In advance, prepare a chart like the one shown and post it in an easily visible classroom location. Share *Caps for Sale: A Tale of a Peddler, Some Monkeys, and Their Monkey Business* by Esphyr Slobodkina (HarperTrophy, 1987). Write "sale" on the board and underline the -ale word family. Have students brainstorm other -ale words and list their suggestions. Then try a display idea that's guaranteed to sell your students on the -ale word family!

First, each student makes three construction paper cap cutouts, using a provided template if desired. He labels each one with a different -ale word. For each cap, the youngster refers to the posted chart, determines the cost of the word, and then writes the price on the cap. After each student reads his words aloud, mount the caps on a jumbo paper tree that has been posted on a board titled "Words for Sale!" Then recognize each youngster with a badge labeled "Top Salesperson."

Prices	
-ale	3¢
b	2¢
d	1¢
m	4¢
p	5¢
sc	6¢

pale 8¢

scale 9¢

BUILD SKILLS

Here's a whale of a skill-building booklet project! Give each student one 5" x 18" white construction paper strip and two gray construction paper copies of the whale pattern (page 13). To make a booklet, a youngster accordion-folds the strip into four equal sections. She cuts out the whales and then glues one whale to each end of the booklet as shown on page 13 (the last page will cover the face on the back cover). On each booklet page, the youngster writes and illustrates a sentence with an -ale word. She glues a wisp of cotton to her front cover to represent the whale's spout of water. Each student, in turn, reads her book aloud to the class. Then she stands it on a table that has been covered with blue paper to represent the ocean. What a colossal reading idea!

ADD EXTENSIONS

Reinforce word family skills with these terrific tales!
The Library Dragon by Carmen Agra Deedy (Peachtree Publishers, 1994)
Rainbow Fish and the Big Blue Whale by Marcus Pfister (North-South Books Inc., 1998)
Little Penguin's Tale by Audrey Wood (Voyager Books, 1993)

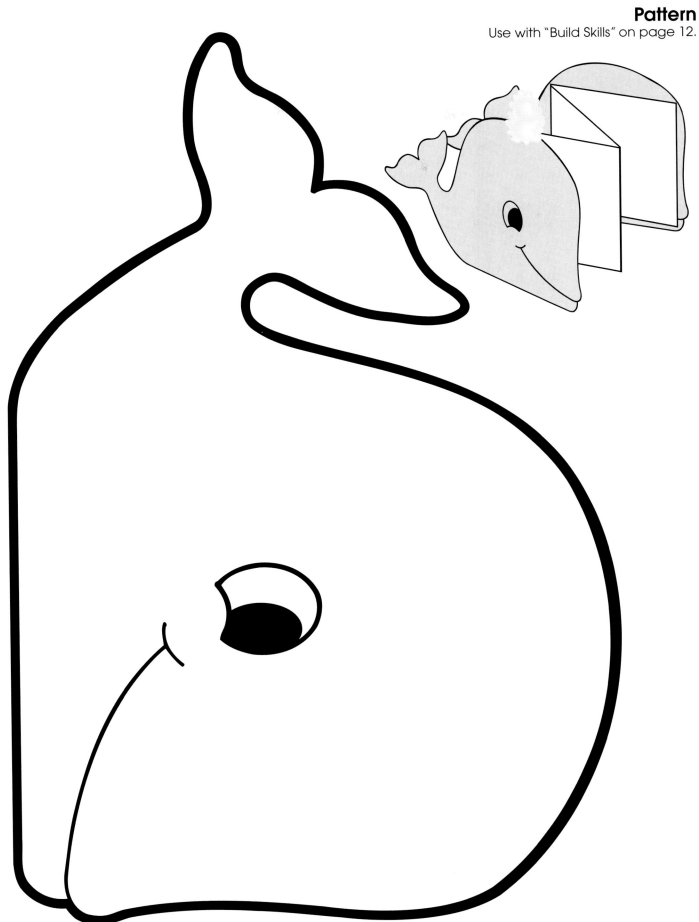

-ame

became

blame

came

fame

flame

frame

games

name

nickname

same

shame

tame

SET THE FOUNDATION

Stretch your young paleontologists' creativity *and* word family skills with this class book project! After a shared reading of *If the Dinosaurs Came Back* by Bernard Most (Harcourt Brace & Company, 1989), write "came" on the board and underline the *-ame* word family. Ask youngsters to name other *-ame* words. With students' help, list each word and underline the *-ame* word family in each one.

To prepare students for using these words in a class version of Most's imaginative tale, label a sheet of chart paper "If the dinosaurs came back..." Have students brainstorm phrases that complete the sentence and include a listed *-ame* word. List the phrases on the chart paper. To make a page for the class book, a student selects a phrase. On a sheet of story paper, he writes a sentence that begins "If the dinosaurs came back" and ends with his chosen phrase. After he illustrates his work, bind all of the students' pages in a book titled "What Would Happen If the Dinosaurs Came Back?" Now that's a "dino-mite" addition to your classroom library!

BUILD SKILLS

These frames are custom-made for *-ame* words! Give each student a copy of page 15. After each student adds the finishing touches to the Word Family Museum by completing the sheet, invite her to create an *-ame* word museum of her own. To do so, she uses crayons to list her favorite *-ame* words on a 7" x 10" sheet of white paper. Then she frames the list by mounting it on a 9" x 12" sheet of colored construction paper. The youngster uses provided arts-and-crafts supplies to decorate her frame as desired. Display students' word family masterpieces on a bulletin board titled "These Words Became Art!"

ADD EXTENSIONS

Use these popular titles to complement your *-ame* word family study.
Chrysanthemum by Kevin Henkes (Mulberry Books, 1996)
What Game Shall We Play? by Pat Hutchins (Mulberry Books, 1995)
A My Name Is... by Alice Lyne (Whispering Coyote Press, 1997)

The Word Family Museum

Use the Word Bank to complete the sentences.
Draw a line under the word family in each word.
Color the frames.

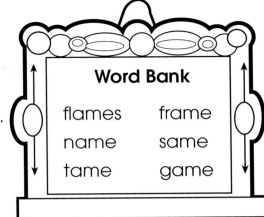

Word Bank

flames	frame
name	same
tame	game

1. I neatly write my _____ on my paper.

2. My baby picture is in a wooden _____ .

3. I have the _____ color hat as you!

4. There are _____ in the fireplace.

5. The circus trainers will _____ the lions.

6. On Saturday, I will play a _____ with my friends.

Bonus Box: Draw a large picture frame on the back of this sheet. Choose one sentence from above. Illustrate it inside the frame.

Note to the teacher: Use with "Build Skills" on page 14.

-an

can

fan

fantastic

Jan

man

pancake

plan

ran

scan

tan

than

van

SET THE FOUNDATION

Try this tempting -an word family idea! Share *The Gingerbread Man* by Eric A. Kimmel (Holiday House, Inc.; 1994) and then display a poster-sized gingerbread man cutout labeled "-an." After verifying that students recognize the word family, ask them to listen for -an words as you reread the book's refrain. After students recall the words, record them on the cutout. Add other brainstormed words to the list; then have each youngster make a batch of -an word gingerbread men.

To do so, each student accordion-folds a 6" x 18" strip of brown construction paper into four equal sections. He traces a gingerbread man template on the folded paper as shown. The youngster cuts out the tracing, being careful not to cut where the hands meet the edges of the paper. Then he unfolds the paper, labels each gingerbread man with a different -an word, and uses construction paper scraps to add decorations. These words look good enough to eat!

BUILD SKILLS

Concentrate on -an words with this partner activity! Give each student a copy of page 17. The youngster initials one corner of each card for easy identification later, then colors and cuts out the cards. She combines her cards with her partner's, shuffles all of them, and places them in a stack.

To begin, one player places the cards facedown in rows on a playing surface. Then each player, in turn, turns two cards over. If she can make an -an word, she arranges the cards to form the word, reads the word aloud, and keeps the cards. If she cannot, she turns the cards back over. The game continues until all of the cards have been paired. The player with the greater number of pairs wins.

ADD EXTENSIONS

This unique version of tic-tac-toe makes students word family winners! Pair students. Give each pair ten blank cards and each partner a different-colored crayon. Each twosome programs its cards with -an words and draws a large tic-tac-toe grid on provided paper. The partners shuffle the cards and stack them facedown. Alternating turns, each partner takes the top card, reads the word aloud, and writes it in a grid space. Play continues until one player writes three words in a horizontal, vertical, or diagonal row and is declared the winner or until all of the spaces have been filled and the game is declared a draw.

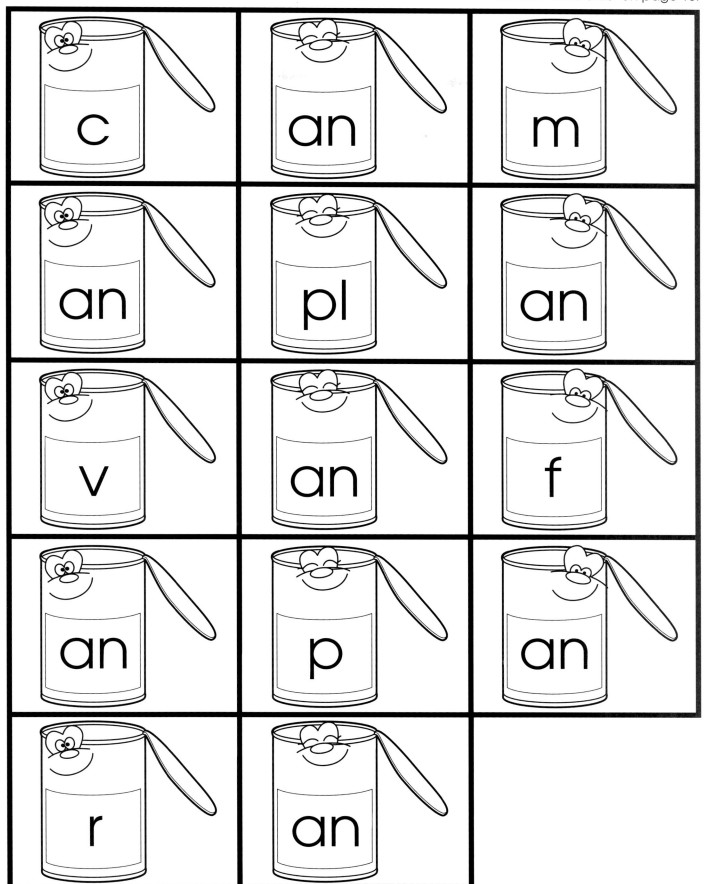

-ank

bank

blank

clank

Frank

rank

sank

shrank

snowbank

tank

thank

thankful

SET THE FOUNDATION

Here's a "fin-tastic" introduction to the *-ank* word family! Draw a large rectangle on the chalkboard to represent a fish tank. Program several fish cutouts with *-ank* words and use magnetic or masking tape to adhere each fish to the tank. Say the rhyme shown on page 19; then encourage students to join in as you read each fish in the tank. Next, remove the fish from the tank and randomly distribute them to students. Ask each student who has a fish to read it aloud and return it to the tank. Then repeat the rhyme and reading process with the entire class.

Next, give each student a copy of page 19. To make his own tankful of fishy words, a student programs each fish with a different *-ank* word, lightly colors it, and then cuts it out. The youngster uses construction paper scraps to make desired fish tank decorations, then glues the fish and decorations onto a 9" x 12" sheet of blue construction paper. With adult assistance, he staples a sheet of waxed paper across his resulting tank, trims any excess waxed paper, and then glues a construction paper frame in place as shown. Have each student take his project and a copy of the poem home to share with his family.

BUILD SKILLS

Bank on this handy language arts idea to reap dividends! Each student folds a 9" x 12" sheet of construction paper in half and then staples several sheets of white paper inside. With the fold at the top, the youngster decorates the resulting cover to resemble a bank and labels it "My -ank Word Bank." When she sees an *-ank* word in a book, a magazine, or other reading material, she "makes a deposit" in her word bank by copying the word onto a blank page. Then, on the same page, she writes and illustrates a sentence that uses the word. For a fun variation, challenge students to find *-ank* words in discarded magazines and newspapers, cut them out, and glue them into their banks. Now that's a valuable reading and writing reference!

ADD EXTENSIONS

Look for the *-ank* word family in these kid-pleasing books!
Who Sank the Boat? by Pamela Allen (PaperStar, 1996)
I'm Thankful Each Day! by P. K. Hallinan (Ideals Children's Books, 1998)
I Miss Franklin P. Shuckles by Ulana Snihura (Annick Press Ltd., 1998)

A Fishy Family
This fish tank is special as you can see.
It holds fish from the **-ank** family.
Reading the words is a lot of fun.
Listen to me read each and every one!

bank   thank   shrank

-ap

apple

cap

clap

flap

happy

lap

map

nap

snap

strap

tap

trap

SET THE FOUNDATION

Uncap loads of word family fun with this booklet idea! Write "-ap" on the board. After reading this word family aloud, add the letter c to make *cap.* Chorally read the word with students. Then write and chorally read several other -ap words.

Next, give each youngster one copy each of the booklet base and cover, along with three copies of the booklet page on page 21. To complete his booklet, the student colors the cover and cap brim. Then he signs the brim and cuts out the patterns. The youngster stacks his cover atop the pages and staples them to the base where indicated. On each page, he writes and illustrates a different -ap word. Encourage each student to reveal what's under his cap by sharing his booklet with a classmate.

BUILD SKILLS

This writing reference is ripe for the picking! Share *The Apple Pie Tree* by Zoe Hall (The Blue Sky Press, 1996), a story about two children who enjoy the apple tree in their yard throughout the year. Write *apple* on a sheet of chart paper and underline *ap.* Point out that this word family can be anywhere in a word. With students' help, write additional words that have -ap in the beginning, middle, or end. Have volunteers underline *ap* in each one.

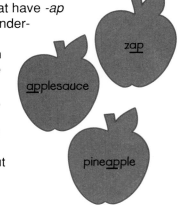

To follow up, mount a poster-sized tree cutout on a bulletin board titled "Pick Some -ap Words!" Have each student write an -ap word on an apple cutout. Ask each youngster, in turn, to read his word aloud, use it in an original sentence, and then mount it on the tree. Add construction paper leaves. Next, have each student imagine that there is an apple tree in his yard. Ask him to write and illustrate a story about it, including three or more words from the display.

ADD EXTENSIONS

It's a snap to fit this word family activity into your busy schedule! Think of a direction for students to follow that uses one of these words: *clap, snap,* or *tap.* Say the -ap word aloud, segmenting it as shown. Have students chorally repeat the word parts and then blend them to pronounce the word. Announce the direction. After students successfully follow it, continue with a desired number of additional directions in a like manner.

Teacher: "Sn-ap."
Students: "Sn-ap. Snap."
Teacher: "Snap your fingers three
times."

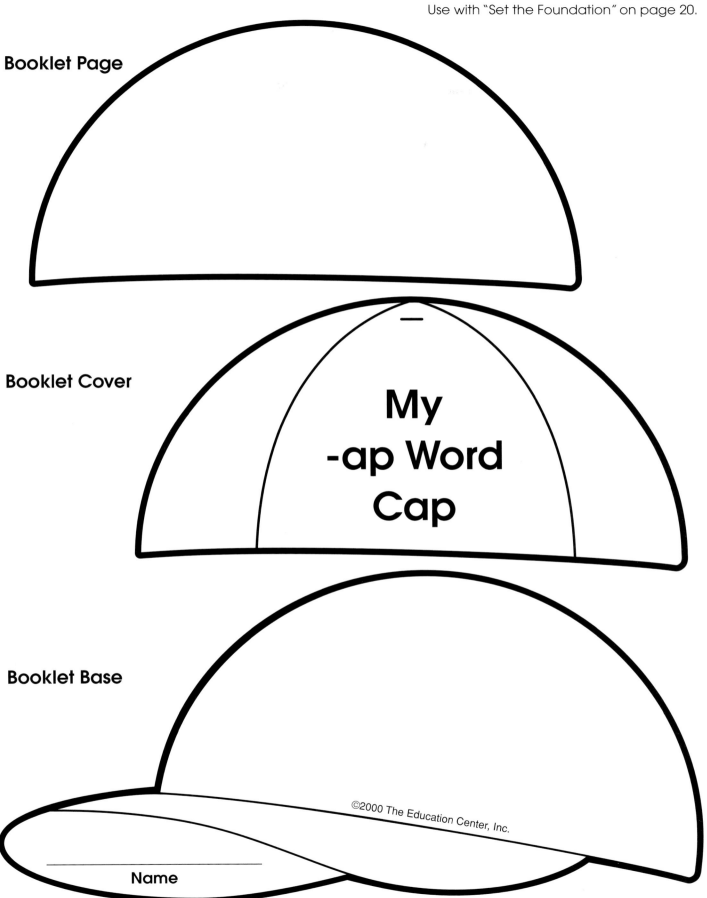

Booklet Page

Booklet Cover

My
-ap Word
Cap

Booklet Base

©2000 The Education Center, Inc.

_____
Name

-ash

cash

crash

dash

eyelash

flash

hash

mash

rash

smash

splash

trash

SET THE FOUNDATION

Dive right in to the -ash word family! Cover a bulletin board with light and dark blue paper to represent the sky and a swimming pool. Add the title "Make a Splash With Words!" Read aloud *Splash!* by Ann Jonas (Greenwillow Books, 1995). Show students the book's front cover as you conceal the first three letters of the title. Help students read the rest of the word. Reveal the letter *l* and read the resulting word with students; then reveal and read the entire word. After writing a student-generated list of -ash words, have students create this splashy display.

Each youngster traces a paper-doll template on skin-toned construction paper. He cuts out the tracing, uses construction paper scraps and crayons to add details so that the cutout resembles a swimmer, and then labels it with a chosen -ash word. Attach the swimmers to the board and invite students to make and add construction paper pool-toy cutouts. To complete the display, add letter cutouts to spell the word *splash* in a few areas of the board, using Jonas's illustrations as a model.

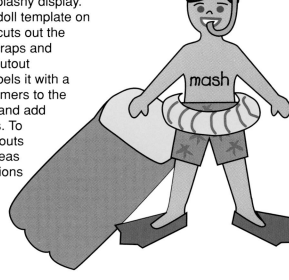

BUILD SKILLS

This flip booklet idea is sure to be a smashing success! To make a booklet, each student stacks five 2" x 3" pieces of paper atop the left side of a 3" x 6" piece of paper. He staples the entire stack at the top. With his resulting booklet closed, the youngster writes -ash on the right side of the last page. The student uses the following initial letters and blends to program each page: *c, cr, l, m, sm,* and *tr.* He reads the word formed by the top page and the last page to himself. The student turns the top page and reads the new word revealed. He continues in a like manner until he has read the entire book, then reads the book to a partner and orally uses each word in a sentence.

ADD EXTENSIONS

Students pick up -ash word writing practice with this reproducible activity! Distribute a copy of page 23 to each student. In the box provided on each trash can, the youngster writes an -ash word that begins with the corresponding letter(s). Then she uses two of the words in original sentences at the bottom of the sheet. For a related follow-up, share *Trashy Town* by Andrea Zimmerman (HarperCollins Children's Books, 1999).

Name _____

Word Family Cleanup

Follow your teacher's directions.
Color the pictures.

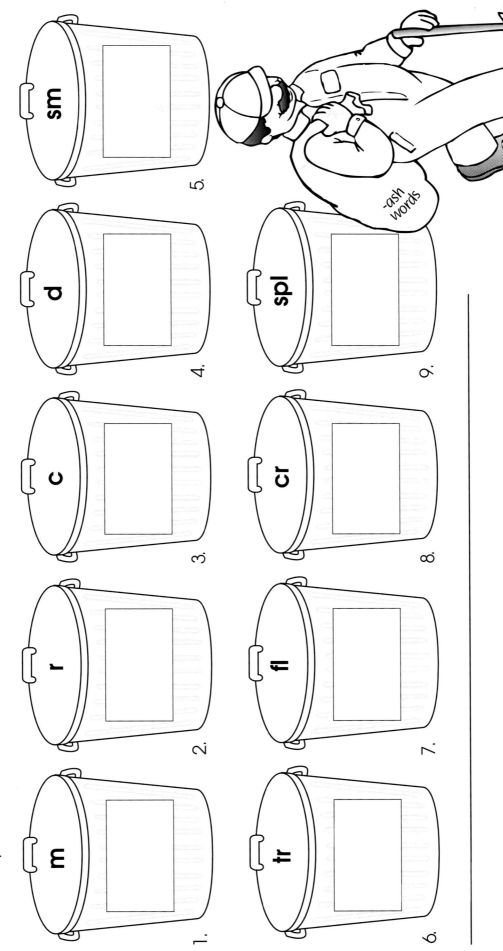

1. m

2. r

3. c

4. d

5. sm

6. tr

7. fl

8. cr

9. spl

-ash words

©2000 The Education Center, Inc. • Word Family Fun • TEC3103 • Key p. 95

Note to the teacher: Use with "Add Extensions" on page 22.

-at

acrobat

bat

cat

doormat

fat

flat

hat

mat

pat

rat

sat

that

SET THE FOUNDATION

Looking for the "purr-fect" introduction to the -at word family? Try this! Share *This and That* by Julie Sykes (Farrar, Straus & Giroux, Inc.; 1998), a delightful tale about a mother cat. Point out that Cat could use some yarn balls to entertain her offspring. Then follow up with this kitty-pleasing mobile project.

To begin, write "cat" and "that" on the board. Ask students what they notice about the words. Lead them to conclude that they are in the -at word family. Brainstorm additional -at words. Next, give each student one white construction paper copy of page 25 and three nine-inch yarn lengths. The youngster writes an -at word on each ball, colors and cuts out the balls and cat, and then uses tape to assemble the mobile as shown on page 25. To complete his project, he hole-punches the cat where indicated and threads a yarn length through the hole to make a hanger.

BUILD SKILLS

Batter up! Stack 12 or more cards that have been programmed with -at words. To prepare for an -at baseball game, designate places for home plate and first, second, and third bases in a large open area. Divide the class into two teams.

To play, have one player stand at home plate and show her a card. If she reads the word correctly, she advances to first base. If she does not, her turn is over. Play continues with the remaining batters on the team, each player advancing one base for each correct word and each team earning a point when a player crosses home plate. (Reshuffle the cards as necessary.) Then the second team "comes to bat." The higher-scoring team wins. Play ball!

ADD EXTENSIONS

Follow up a reading of *That's Good! That's Bad!* by Margery Cuyler (Owlet, 1993) with this critical-thinking activity. Program each of several sentence strips with a sentence that has an -at word and describes an event. Chorally read each sentence, in turn; then have a volunteer underline the -at word.

Next, each student labels a card "That's good" and another card "That's bad." Remind students that events can be viewed in either a positive or negative light. Read a sentence aloud and ask each youngster to show the card he thinks tells about the event. Invite students to share their reasoning. Repeat with the remaining sentences. Then, on provided paper, have each student expand and illustrate his favorite sentence using the book as a model.

My uncle stepped on my hat!

My uncle stepped on my hat! That's bad! No, that's good! He felt sorry and bought a book for me.

-ate

crate

date

gate

grate

Kate

late

locate

Nate

plate

rate

skateboard

states

SET THE FOUNDATION

When it comes to building -ate words, this game can't be beat! Obtain one set of programmable wooden or plastic cubes for every three students. Program half the cubes with the following: d, gr, l, pl, r, and st. Write "-ate" on every side of each remaining cube. Read Kate Skates by Jane O'Connor (Grosset & Dunlap, Inc.; 1995) aloud; then direct students' attention to the title. Ask youngsters what they notice. Lead them to conclude that "Kate" and "Skates" are both in the -ate word family. Brainstorm other -ate words; then divide students into groups of three for word-building fun.

To begin, give each student a sheet of paper and have him number it from 1 to 5. Give each group one of each type of cube. Each player, in turn, rolls the cubes and arranges them to form a word. He reads the word aloud and writes it on his paper. Play continues until each player has written five words. He earns two points for each word that he listed only once and one point for each word that he listed more than once. The highest-scoring player wins.

Helen

1. date
2. plate
3.
4.
5.

BUILD SKILLS

Serve up word family practice with this enticing partner game! Program each of 15 cards with an -ate word and 5 cards with words that are not from the -ate word family. Scramble the cards, put them in a large plastic bowl, and then stack two paper plates nearby. To play, each player places a plate in front of herself. The players position the bowl between them. Each player, in turn, takes a card without looking inside the bowl. She reads the word aloud. If it is an -ate word, she puts it on her plate. If it is not, she places it in a discard pile. Play continues until the bowl is empty. The player with the fuller plate wins!

ADD EXTENSIONS

This reproducible activity puts -ate words on the map! Ask students to name the state in which their school is located and help them find it on a United States map. Give each youngster a copy of page 27. Explain that the sentences tell about a family that is moving out of state. After each student follows the directions to complete the sheet, encourage him to do the Bonus Box activity. To extend the activity for older students, share The Scrambled States of America by Laurie Keller (Henry Holt and Company, Inc.; 1998).

On the Move

Use the Word Bank to complete each sentence.

1. We are going to move to a different _____.

2. I want to live where I can _____ on a frozen lake.

3. My sister _____ wants to live where it is cold.

4. Dad wants to live in a house with a fence and a _____.

5. Mom wants us to live close to school so we will never be _____.

6. Do you think we can _____ a place like that?

Word Bank

skate	gate
locate	state
Kate	late

Bonus Box: Think about the story above. On the back of this sheet, draw a picture of a new home that would make everyone happy.

-aw

awful

claw

draw

drawing

flaw

jaw

law

paws

saw

straw

strawberry

thaw

SET THE FOUNDATION

Get your -aw word family study off to a "berry" good start! Make a strawberry-shaped tracer and use it to make a class set of white booklet pages and two red construction paper covers. Decorate one cover to resemble a strawberry and label it "If I Had a Red Ripe Strawberry…" Read aloud *The Little Mouse, the Red Ripe Strawberry, and the Big Hungry Bear* by Audrey Wood (Child's Play [International] Ltd, 1990). Display the embellished construction paper cover and ask a student to underline the -aw word family in "Strawberry." Then write a student-generated list of other -aw words on the back of the cover for later reference.

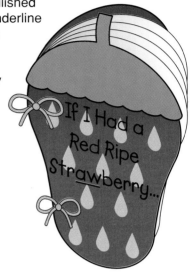

Next, discuss the ideas the mouse in the story had for keeping his strawberry. Give each student a strawberry-shaped page and ask her to write and illustrate her ideas about what *she* would do if she had a strawberry. Bind students' completed pages between the covers. Now that's an enticing addition to your classroom library!

BUILD SKILLS

Here's a game that draws on students' knowledge of the -aw word family. Give each student one copy of page 29 and have him cut apart the word cards at the bottom of the sheet. Instruct the student to randomly glue his cards onto the lotto board at the top of the sheet. Prepare an additional set of cards and place the cards in a container. Then give each youngster 12 game markers.

To play, take a card from the container and read the word aloud. Have each student place a game marker on the corresponding paw on his board. Continue play until one student has placed a game marker on every paw in one row. Verify his words and declare him the winner. Then ask students to clear their boards for another round.

ADD EXTENSIONS

Music and movement energize this word identification activity! Prepare a class supply of -aw word cards, using words more than once as necessary. Have students sit with their chairs in a circle. Distribute the cards and have each student, in turn, read his card aloud. Next, ask each youngster to stand and place his card on his chair. Instruct students to walk clockwise around the circle when music is playing. Start the music and then stop it after a few moments. Have each student pick up the card on the chair closest to him and read it aloud. Resume play by restarting the music. Continue for a desired number of rounds.

Name_____

Playful Paws

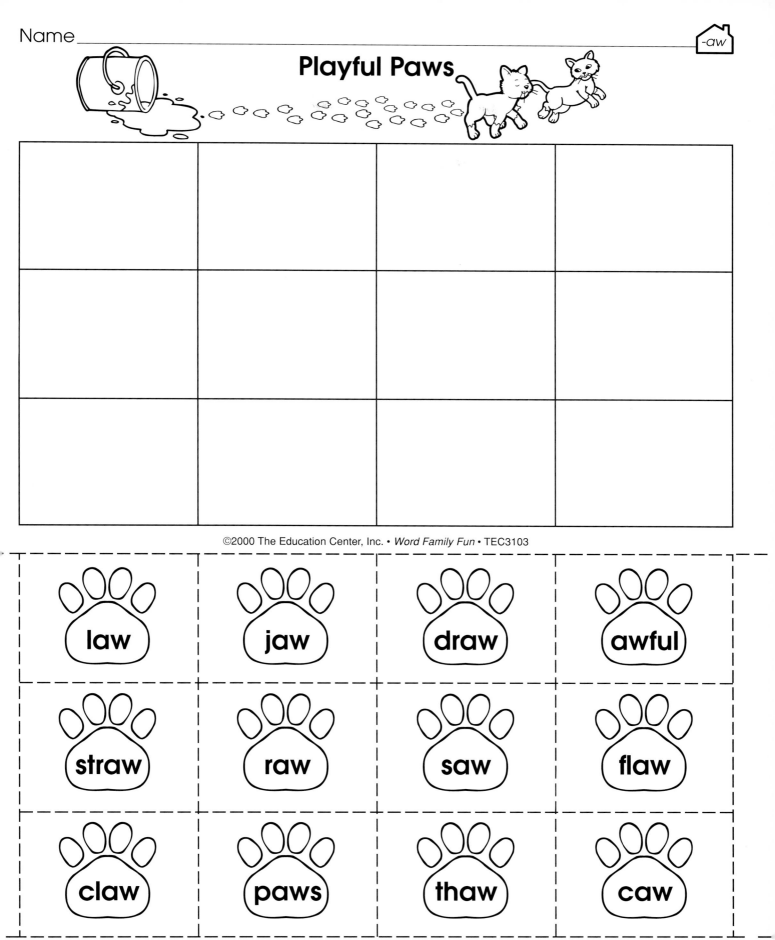

©2000 The Education Center, Inc. • *Word Family Fun* • TEC3103

law jaw draw awful

straw raw saw flaw

claw paws thaw caw

Note to the teacher: Use with "Build Skills" on page 28.

29

-ay

bay

clay

day

gray

hay

pay

play

spray

stay

today

tray

way

©2000 The Education Center, Inc.

SET THE FOUNDATION

Introduce the *-ay* word family down by the bay! Share *Down by the Bay* from the Raffi Songs to Read® series (Crown Publishers, Inc.; 1990). Display a card for each of the following: *ay, b, d, gr, h, l, m, p, pl, r,* and *s.* Explain that two of the cards can be used to form the word *bay.* To demonstrate, have a student hold the *-ay* card at the front of the class. Invite another youngster to choose the appropriate card and then hold it next to the first student to form *bay.* After the class chorally reads the word, invite different youngsters to form other *-ay* words in a similar manner. Then create a bayside word reference with this display idea.

Give each student a light blue construction paper bird cutout and have him label it with an *-ay* word of his choice. Staple students' birds onto a board that has been decorated with layers of blue paper to resemble a bay. Along the edges of the board, add twisted paper strips for vines and student-made paper watermelons. To complete the display, add a poster with the question "Did You Ever See -ay Words Flying With Jaybirds Down by the Bay?"

BUILD SKILLS

What's in the cards? Loads of word-building practice! Give each student a construction paper copy of page 31. Have her cut out the cards and tray. Help her assemble the tray as illustrated. Pair students. Instruct each player to place her *-ay* card faceup in front of herself on the playing surface and stack her remaining cards facedown nearby.

To begin, each player, in turn, draws three cards from her stack and stands them in her tray. She chooses one or more of the cards to make a word with her *-ay* card. She reads the word aloud and writes it on provided paper. Then she draws one card from the stack for each letter card that she has used and stands it in the tray. Play continues with each player making words as described and drawing replacement cards as possible until each player has used as many of her cards as she can. Now that's a letter-perfect skill-building idea!

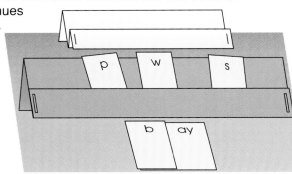

ADD EXTENSIONS

Sharing these books is a great way to reinforce the *-ay* word family!
Today Is Monday by Eric Carle (PaperStar, 1997)
I Went to the Bay by Ruth Miller (Kids Can Press Ltd., 1999)
Five Little Ducks from the Raffi Songs to Read® series (Crown Publishers, Inc.; 1992)

30

Cards

t	d	l	s	w	m	h
r	b	s	p	l		ay

Tray

-eat

beat

cheat

eating

heat

heater

meat

meatball

neat

repeat

seat

treats

wheat

SET THE FOUNDATION

What's on the menu? A hearty word family introduction! To prepare, enlarge and color a copy of the frog pattern on page 33 to make a poster-sized frog. Use a craft knife to carefully cut along the dotted lines; then gently pull the frog's hands forward. If desired, glue on a paper napkin (see the illustration). Display the frog below the title "Welcome to the -eat Word Café!" To make a menu for the frog, cut a piece of heavy paper to fit his arm span. Fold the paper in half, and label the outside "Menu of -eat Words."

To begin, share the pop-up book *I Love to Eat Bugs!* by John Strejan (Könemann, 1999). Then direct students' attention to the frog display. Explain that just like the frog in the book, this frog has a big appetite. But he doesn't love to eat bugs; he loves to eat words—especially -eat words! As students brainstorm -eat words, list them on the outside of the menu. Have student volunteers underline the -eat word family in each word and then use markers to add a decorative border to the menu. Use a stapler to attach the menu to the display as shown. Encourage youngsters to refer to this froggy diner's menu throughout your word family study.

BUILD SKILLS

This reading activity is a real treat! Give each student one copy of the rhyme and two copies of each of the four treats on page 33. Read the rhyme with students. Each youngster writes an -eat word on every treat, colors the treats, and then cuts out the treats and rhyme. The youngster glues the rhyme onto a paper lunch bag and personalizes the bag as desired. Then she places the treats inside the bag.

After every student has prepared her bag of word treats, lead students in chorally reading the rhyme. Invite one student to remove her treats from her bag and read each word aloud. Pair students. Then have each youngster read the poem and share her word treats with her partner in a like manner.

ADD EXTENSIONS

When it comes to reinforcing the -eat word family, these books can't be beat! *The Little Red Hen* by Byron Barton (HarperCollins Children's Books, 1994) *The Seven Silly Eaters* by Mary Ann Hoberman (Browndeer Press, 1997) *Gregory, the Terrible Eater* by Mitchell Sharmat (Scholastic Inc., 1989)

Rhyme and Treats
Use with "Build Skills" on page 32.

Word Treats

I have some treats for you to see.
They are from the **-eat** family.

Making them was a lot of fun.
Now I will read them, one by one.

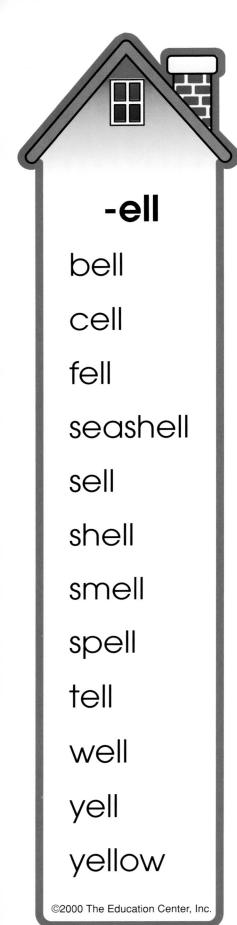

-ell

bell

cell

fell

seashell

sell

shell

smell

spell

tell

well

yell

yellow

SET THE FOUNDATION

Introduce the -ell word family with this unique twist on a traditional song. Program a card for each of the following words: *bell, dell, fell, sell, shell, swell,* and *yell.* Read *The Farmer in the Dell* by Alexandra Wallner (Holiday House, Inc.; 1998) aloud; then lead the class in singing the song as you show the corresponding book illustrations.

To prepare students to write a new version of the song that's filled with -ell words, point out the word *dell* on the cover. Cover the initial letter and invite a student to identify the word family. Then, for each prepared card, have a different volunteer read the word aloud and underline the word family. With students' help, create an original verse of "The Farmer in the Dell" for each word and then write it on chart paper. After students find and underline every -ell word on the chart, lead your young songwriters in singing their toe-tapping, skill-building song.

BUILD SKILLS

What "shell" students do to practice word family skills? This seashell project is just the thing! Give each student a copy of page 35. Have her color and cut out the seashell; then help her cut two horizontal slits where indicated. To assemble her project, the student cuts out the letter strip and threads it through the slits in the seashell. She glues the ends of the strip together to form a ring as shown on page 35. To form a word, the student turns the ring until one letter or blend is visible between the slits. Pair students and have each youngster read the words to her partner. Then, on provided paper, ask each student to write and illustrate a sentence with her favorite -ell word.

ADD EXTENSIONS

Students will chime right in with -ell words during this mystery word activity! On each of several sentence strips, write a different sentence that has an -ell word. Tape the top of a bell cutout to each sentence so that the cutout covers the -ell word. Tell students that all of the hidden words are in the -ell word family. Display each sentence, in turn, and invite a student to read it aloud, saying "blank" when he comes to the bell cutout. Encourage students to use context clues to determine what -ell word would make sense in the sentence. After students share their ideas, lift the bell to reveal the mystery word.

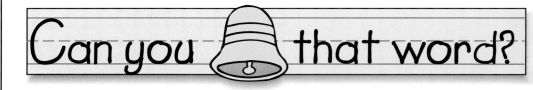

Can you 🔔 that word?

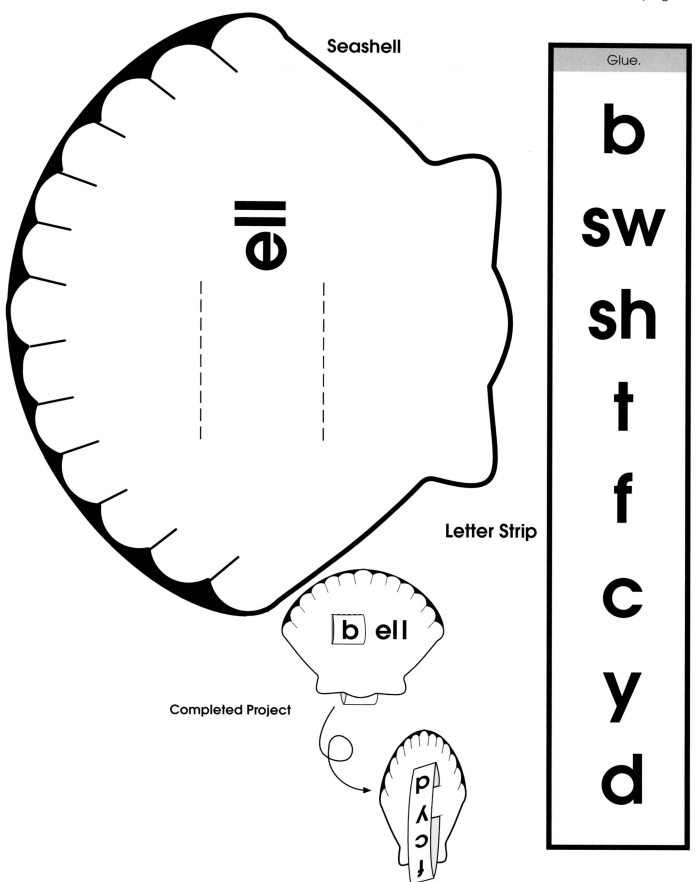

Seashell

ell

Letter Strip

Glue.

b

sw

sh

t

f

c

y

d

Completed Project

b ell

-est

best

chest

contest

crest

forest

jest

nest

pest

resting

test

vest

west

©2000 The Education Center, Inc.

SET THE FOUNDATION

It's no contest—one of the best ways to introduce the -est word family is to read *The Treasure Chest* by Dominique Falda (North-South Books Inc., 1999). After a first reading, instruct your students to listen for -est words as you reread the book. To follow up, use magnetic letters on a display board to form the word *chest,* and read the word with students. Replace the magnetic *c* and *h* with a *t* and have a student volunteer read the resulting word. Then, with students' help, use the letters to form these additional words: *best, jest, nest, pest, rest, vest,* and *west.*

Next, tell students that each of them will make a treasure chest like Squirrel's, except that their chests will be filled with -est words. To make his chest, each child folds and staples a 12" x 18" sheet of construction paper as shown. Then he uses a variety of arts-and-crafts materials to decorate it as desired. Next, the youngster cuts -est words from a discarded magazine or newspaper. He glues each one on a 6" x 8" piece of construction paper. After he compiles a list of several -est words, invite him to read the words to a partner and then slip the list into the treasure chest for safekeeping!

BUILD SKILLS

This nest is sure to hatch a batch of word family practice! Give a copy of page 37 to each student. Instruct the child to color and cut out the birds and the nest. Next, have her cut out the wheel and use a brad to fasten it to the back of the nest as illustrated on page 37. Direct the youngster to turn the wheel and read each word aloud. Then tell her to slowly turn the wheel again, write each of the six words on a different bird, and glue the birds on the nest. Encourage her to take her nest full of word birds home to share with her family.

ADD EXTENSIONS

Looking for more books with -est words? Check out these great titles!
The Magpies' Nest by Joanna Foster (Clarion Books, 1995)
Great Aunt Martha by Rebecca C. Jones (Dutton Children's Books, 1995)
The Jester Has Lost His Jingle by David Saltzman (The Jester Company, Inc.; 1995)

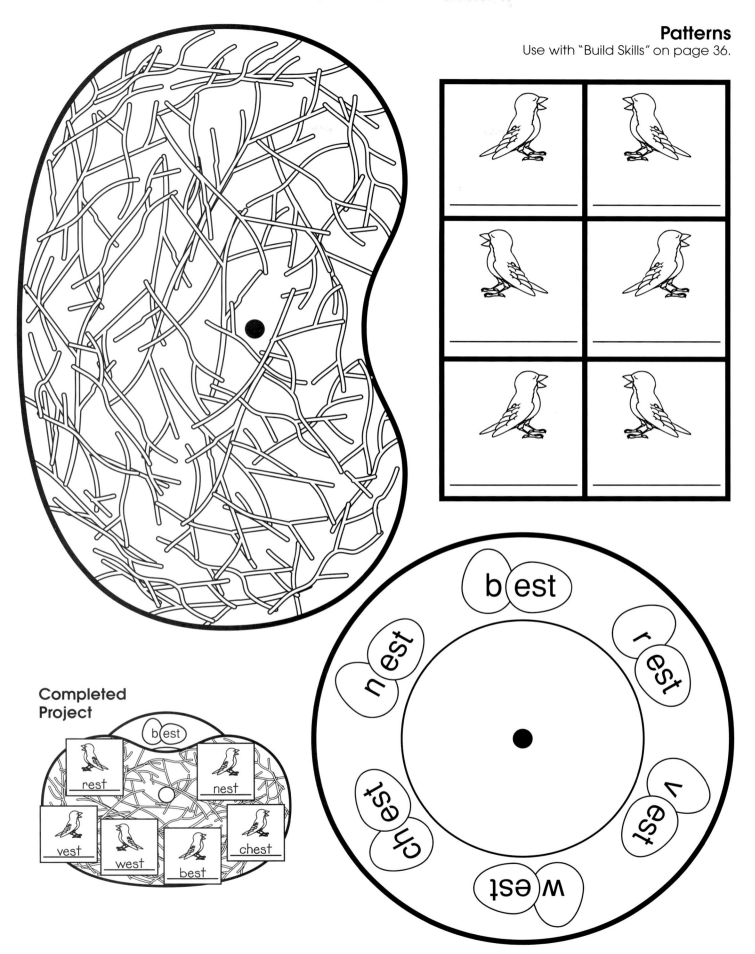

Completed Project

-ice

advice

dice

ice

mice

nice

price

rice

slice

spice

spiced

twice

 # SET THE FOUNDATION

Read it once; read it twice. Read *Chicken Soup With Rice: A Book of Months* by Maurice Sendak (HarperTrophy, 1991) to introduce *-ice* words! First, make a soup can cutout from a 12" x 18" sheet of paper. Write "Chicken Soup With Rice" at the bottom of the cutout and "ice" at the top as illustrated. Cut two horizontal slits to the left of "-ice" as shown. Then make a 20-inch-long I-shaped paper strip. Feed the strip through the slits. Program it with the following: *d, m, n, pr, r, sl, sp,* and *tw.* Read the story aloud; then display the prepared cutout. As you pull up the strip, encourage students to read each word revealed. Write the words on the cutout and have student volunteers underline the featured word family in each one.

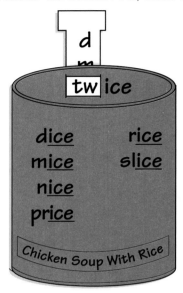

d
m
tw ice

dice   rice
mice   slice
nice
price

Chicken Soup With Rice

 # BUILD SKILLS

Rolling once, rolling twice, rolling for word family practice is nice! Give each student a copy of page 39. Instruct him to color and cut out the die pattern and then cut out the recording sheet. To assemble the die, the student folds the pattern on the dotted lines and glues the flaps together where indicated.

Have each student choose a partner. To play, each student, in turn, rolls his die. He writes the word for the picture he rolled on his recording sheet, referring to the word bank as needed. If a student rolls a picture more than once, he makes a tally mark in the box next to the corresponding word. Partners continue taking turns until each of them has written all six words. Then each twosome uses its tally marks to compare results.

 # ADD EXTENSIONS

Add spice to your word family study with silly sentences! Use a different-colored marker to write each of the following on a separate sentence strip:

The rice had too much spice for the price.
The mice rolled the dice twice.

Cut each sentence apart; then place one set of sentence strip pieces in order in a pocket chart. Read the sentence as a class. Next, scramble the pieces and invite one child to put them in the correct order. Repeat the process with the second sentence. Then invite children to create their own silly *-ice* sentences for more scrambled sentence fun!

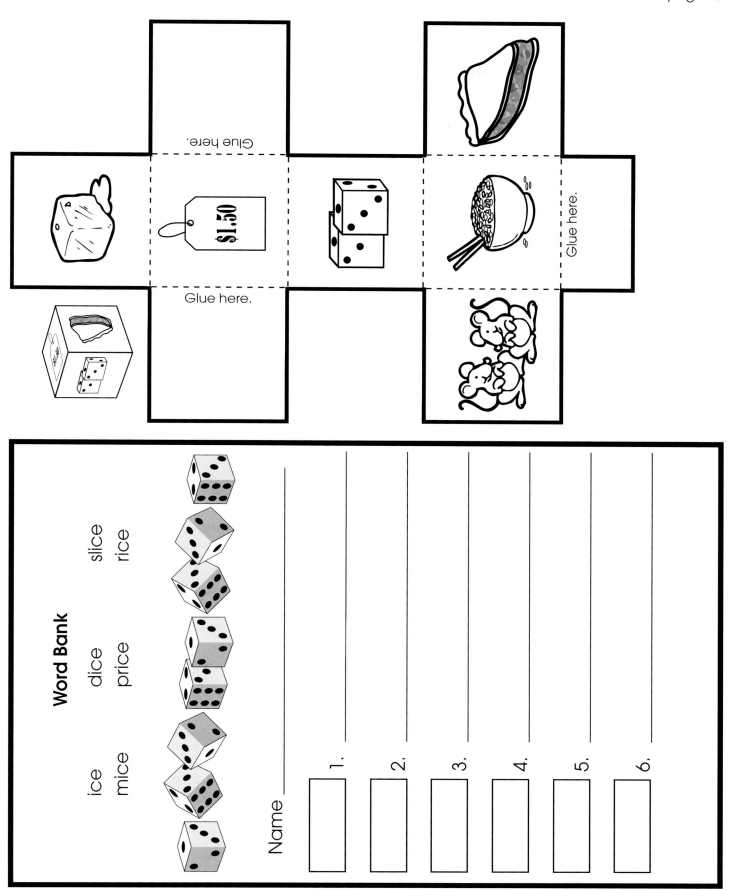

Glue here.

Glue here.

Glue here.

$1.50

Word Bank

slice   rice

dice   price

ice   mice

Name

1.

2.

3.

4.

5.

6.

-ick

brick

chick

drumstick

pick

quick

sick

stick

thick

toothpick

trick

SET THE FOUNDATION

Who better than the eccentric character from *Picky Mrs. Pickle* by Christine M. Schneider (Walker Publishing Company, Inc.; 1999) to help introduce the *-ick* word family? After sharing this humorous book, write "picky" and "pickle" on the board. Point out the *-ick* word family in each word and invite students to name other *-ick* words. Then have each student make a jar of *-ick* words guaranteed to satisfy even Mrs. Pickle's finicky tastes.

To begin, give each student one white construction paper copy of the jar pattern, four to six copies of the pickle patterns (page 41), and one 6" x 9" piece of white construction paper. The youngster labels each pickle with a different *-ick* word and writes his name on the jar. Then he colors and cuts out the pickles and jar. The student staples the jar atop the rectangular piece of construction paper where indicated and trims the paper to the shape of the jar. Then he opens the resulting minibook and glues the pickles inside. Now that's a collection of words that would tickle Mrs. Pickle pink!

BUILD SKILLS

Here's a quick and easy word family center idea! Program one end of each of a number of craft sticks with a different *-ick* word. Stand the sticks, word end down, in a decorative container. Place the container and a supply of paper and pencils in a center. Then arrange for pairs of students to visit the center.

Each student, in turn, takes one stick, reads the word aloud, and places it on a work surface. After all of the sticks have been removed from the container, the students arrange the sticks in categories of their choice, such as words with blends or action words. Each student writes and labels every group of words on a sheet of paper. For a word recognition variation of this activity, prepare two identical sets of sticks and have students use them to play *-ick* word memory.

ADD EXTENSIONS

Help word family skills click with this collection of literature!
Tick-Tock by Eileen Browne (Candlewick Press, 1996)
Flicka, Ricka, Dicka and the Big Red Hen by Maj Lindman (Albert Whitman & Company, 1995)
"Ickle Me, Pickle Me, Tickle Me Too" from *Where the Sidewalk Ends: The Poems and Drawings of Shel Silverstein* by Shel Silverstein (HarperCollins Children's Books, 1974)

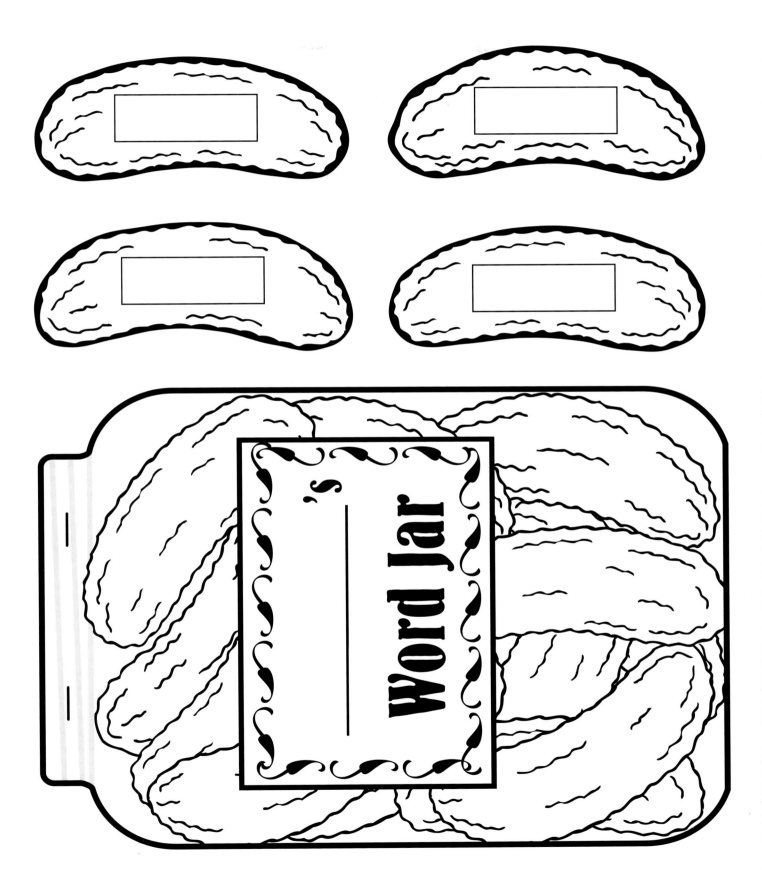

Word Jar

_____'s

-ide

beside

bride

divide

hide

outside

ride

side

slide

tide

wide

 # SET THE FOUNDATION

What's inside this barn? A flock of -ide words! Make a large barn cutout as shown and mount it on a bulletin board that has been covered with white paper. Title the board "Look Inside!"

Share *Inside a Barn in the Country* by Alyssa Satin Capucilli (Scholastic Inc., 1995); then direct students' attention to the display. Write "inside" in the doorway, underline the -ide word family, and read the word with students. As students brainstorm other -ide words, list them in the doorway. Encourage students to practice reading the words throughout your word family study. Invite each youngster who successfully reads all the words to make a paper barnyard critter and add it to the display.

inside

ride
hide
side
beside

 # BUILD SKILLS

Slide right into word family practice with this partner game! Give each student a copy of page 43, a paper clip, and a pencil; then pair students. Demonstrate how to use the spinner on the reproducible page by placing a paper clip in the middle of the spinner, standing a pencil in the clip with one hand, and then spinning the clip with the other.

Partners alternate turns. To take a turn, a partner spins. He uses the letter(s) on which the paper clip lands to complete an -ide word, working from the bottom to the top of the ladder. If he spins letter(s) that he has already used or a letter that cannot be used to make an -ide word, his turn is over. The first partner to reach the top of the ladder wins. After both partners complete all of their words, they illustrate and color their sheets to show playground scenes.

 # ADD EXTENSIONS

Here's an idea that puts your young detectives hot on the trail of -ide words! Use yarn to make a large circle on the classroom floor. Arrange a number of -ide word cards faceup on the floor so that some are inside the circle and some are outside. Gather students around the circle. To begin, secretly choose one of the cards. Have the first student on your left ask a yes-or-no question to help determine the word's identity, such as "Is it inside the circle?" or "Does it have two syllables?" Answer the question and then continue around the circle in a like manner until one student guesses the word. Invite this student to secretly choose a different word for another round of play.

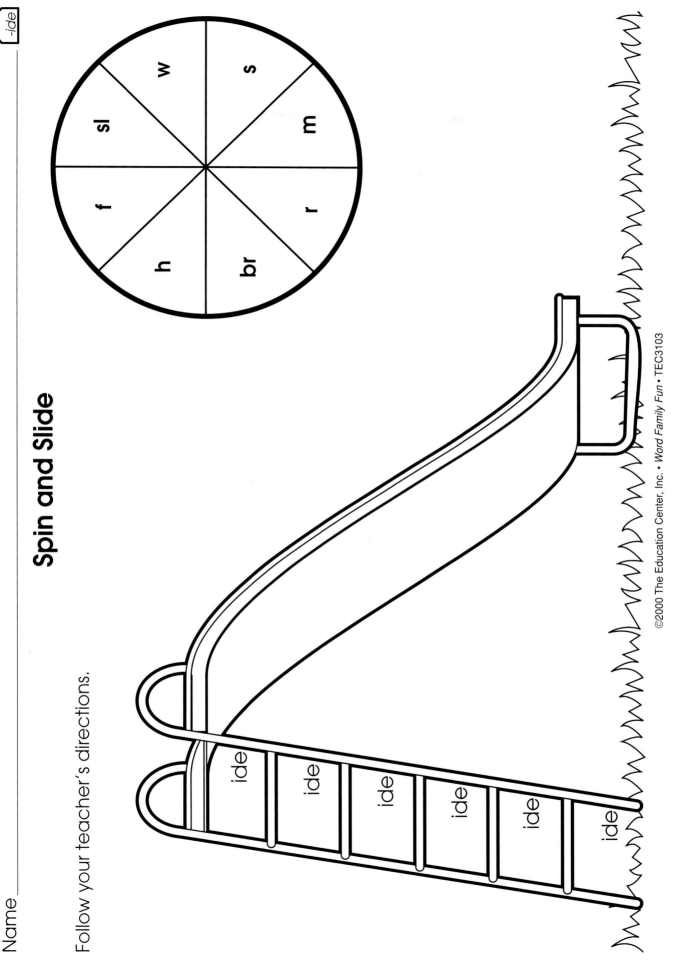

Name _____

-ide

Spin and Slide

Follow your teacher's directions.

Spinner letters: w, s, sl, m, f, r, h, br

Slide steps: ide, ide, ide, ide, ide, ide

©2000 The Education Center, Inc. • Word Family Fun • TEC3103

Note to the teacher: Use with "Build Skills" on page 42.

-ight

bright

fight

flight

frighten

knight

might

nights

right

sight

tight

tonight

twilight

SET THE FOUNDATION

With firefly illustrations that actually light up, *The Very Lonely Firefly* by Eric Carle (Philomel Books, 1995) provides a delightful springboard for an *-ight* word family activity! After reading the story aloud, place a blank transparency on an overhead projector. Use a wipe-off marker to write "light" and "night." Lead students to notice that both words are in the *-ight* word family. As students brainstorm other *-ight* words, list each suggestion; then try this enlightening writing activity.

To begin, each youngster imagines how the story might be different if it were about a very *happy* firefly. On a half sheet of writing paper, he writes two or more sentences about a happy firefly, using at least one *-ight* word in each sentence. The student glues his writing on a sheet of black construction paper. On the blank side of the construction paper, he uses tissue paper scraps to make a firefly illustration, using Carle's collages as a model.

Next, divide students into small groups. Ask each student to read his writing to his group. Have each listener use a yellow or white crayon to draw a small firefly near the reader's firefly. Encourage each student to share his work with his family and then invite each family member to add a firefly to his nighttime illustration.

BUILD SKILLS

Help this knight find his bright and shining armor! Write "night" and "knight" on the board. Lead students in comparing and contrasting the words. After verifying that students know the meaning of *knight,* give each student a copy of page 45. Explain that the knight shown has a problem—he has lost his armor! To help the knight find his armor, the youngster uses a pencil to follow the path of *-ight* words. As she comes to an *-ight* word, she circles the word and writes it on the scroll. If the student completes the maze correctly, the words will be written in the order shown. On the back of the sheet, have the youngster draw a picture of the knight after he found his armor and then add a caption.

Amazing Words

1. night
2. fight
3. light
4. might
5. bright
6. sight
7. flight
8. right

ADD EXTENSIONS

Brighten your word family study with these titles!
Flashlight by Betsy James (Alfred A. Knopf, Inc.; 1997)
Good Night, Gorilla by Peggy Rathmann (G. P. Putnam's Sons, 1994)
Ulaq and the Northern Lights by Harriet Peck Taylor (Farrar, Straus & Giroux, Inc.; 1998)

Out-of-Sight Armor

Follow your teacher's directions.

Amazing Words

1. _____   5. _____

2. _____   6. _____

3. _____   7. _____

4. _____   8. _____

SUPER WORK

dip   sit   try   mint

night

rob   might   bright   sob

fight   light   king   ice

bill

hide

pink   big   sight

lock

flight   cat

boat

fine   right

trip

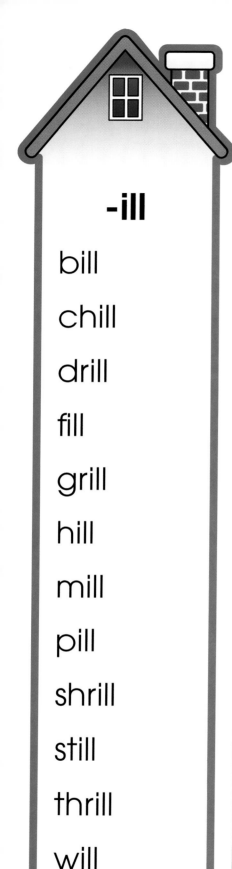

-ill

bill

chill

drill

fill

grill

hill

mill

pill

shrill

still

thrill

will

SET THE FOUNDATION

A climb on this unique hill provides rewarding reading practice! Cover a bulletin board with blue paper and then add a green paper hill as shown. On chart paper, write the poem shown. After leading students in one or more choral readings, underline *hill* in the first verse. Have student volunteers underline *hill* each time it occurs in the poem. As a class, brainstorm other *-ill* words. Write each suggestion on a separate card, mount the cards on the sides of the hill as illustrated, and then lead students in chorally reading them.

For individual skill practice, a student "climbs" the hill by reading each word aloud, beginning on the bottom left side. After a successful climb up one side and down the other, he writes his name in the middle of the hill. Present each young climber with an award ribbon cutout labeled "King of the -ill Word Hill!"

The Race
In a faraway place,
There was a big race,
A race to the top of the hill!

When the flag waved to start,
With joy in my heart,
I ran toward the top of the hill.

But I came to a stop,
And fell with a flop,
Long before the top of the hill.

For this tired athlete
Let's change next year's meet
And start at the *top* of the hill!

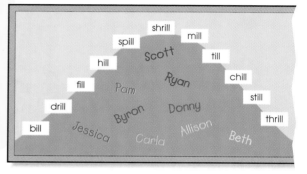

BUILD SKILLS

It's a parade! A caterpillar parade, that is! Give each student one copy of page 47. The youngster cuts out the circles and arranges them on the caterpillars, repositioning the circles as necessary to make an *-ill* word on each one (caution students not to mistake the *d* for a *p*). When the youngster is satisfied with their placement, she glues the circles in place. Read the sentences at the bottom of the reproducible page with students; then have each youngster use the words she made to complete them. For a related creative-writing activity, ask each student to use a specified number of *-ill* words in a story about a silly caterpillar.

ADD EXTENSIONS

Looking for books that reinforce word family skills? These titles fit the bill!
A-Hunting We Will Go! by Steven Kellogg (Morrow Junior Books, 1998)
Nathaniel Willy, Scared Silly by Judith Mathews (Aladdin Paperbacks, 1999)
Silly Sally by Audrey Wood (Harcourt Brace & Company, 1992)

Caterpillar Parade

Follow your teacher's directions.

I saw ten caterpillars crawling up a _____.

They were not moving fast, but they did not stand _____.

Seeing the parade of bugs was really a _____.

It looked just like a caterpillar fire _____!

-in

chin

fin

grin

pin

pumpkin

shin

skin

thin

tin

twin

win

winter

SET THE FOUNDATION

Plant the seeds for word family fun! Program one seed cutout for each of the following: *ch, f, gr, k, p, sk, sp, th, tw,* and *w.* Place the seeds in a plastic pumpkin pail. Next, share *Pumpkin Pumpkin* by Jeanne Titherington (Mulberry Books, 1990). Display a jumbo pumpkin cutout and write "pumpkin" on it. Use a word framer (pattern on page 59) to frame *-in,* concealing the rest of the word; verify that students recognize the word family. Expand the word framer to show *kin,* read it aloud, and then expand it to show *pumpkin.* After students identify the word, ask a volunteer to remove a seed from the pail, name an *-in* word that begins with the letter(s) shown, and then write the word on the pumpkin cutout. Continue with additional volunteers until the pail is empty.

Next, have each student make a construction paper pumpkin cutout. Ask him to use a crayon to write several *-in* words on it and color the stem. Invite each student to orally use one of his words in a sentence before posting the cutout on a bulletin board titled "A Bumper Crop of -in Words!"

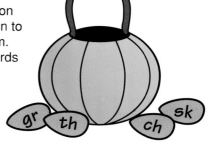

BUILD SKILLS

Students will be seeing double with this word-filled version of Go Fish. Give each student a white construction paper copy of page 49. Have her color and cut out the cards. Divide students into pairs and ask each pair to combine and shuffle its cards.

One player deals five cards to her partner and to herself, then stacks the remaining cards facedown. Each player removes any matching word cards from her hand and sets them aside. Alternating turns, each player chooses one card from her hand, reads it aloud, and asks her partner if she has the card with the same word. If so, the partner gives her the requested card and then the player sets it aside with its match. If not, the player draws one card from the stack and sets aside any resulting matches. Her turn is over when she can make no more matches. Play continues until one player has no cards left. The player with more pairs wins. Collect each student pair's cards. Place them in a resealable plastic bag and store them in a center for additional skill practice.

ADD EXTENSIONS

Check out these winning titles!
Twinnies by Eve Bunting (Harcourt Brace & Company, 1997)
White Wonderful Winter! by Elaine W. Good (Good Books, 1994)
Now I Will Never Leave the Dinner Table by Jane Read Martin and Patricia Marx (HarperCollins Children's Books, 1999)

-ine

dine

fine

lines

mine

nineteen

pine

pineapple

shine

sunshine

twine

valentine

vine

SET THE FOUNDATION

To get your -ine word family study off to a fine start, read *Rise and Shine* by Raffi, Bonnie Simpson, and Bert Simpson (Crown Publishers, Inc.; 1996) aloud. Write "shine" on the board, underline the -ine word family, and chorally read the word with students. After giving each student an individual chalkboard, name another -ine word. Have each youngster write the word on her board and then hold it up. Scan the raised chalkboards to determine students' accuracy. Write the word on the classroom board as a youngster who has written it correctly spells it aloud. Then underline the word family. Continue in a like manner with a desired number of additional -ine words.

To follow up, give each student a paper clip, a game marker, and a copy of page 51. Demonstrate how to use the spinner by placing a paper clip in the middle, standing a pencil in the clip with one hand, and spinning the clip with the other. Pair students and have each twosome put one gameboard aside. To play, each student takes turns spinning, moving her marker as indicated, and then reading aloud the word on which her marker lands. (Her partner provides help as needed.) The first student to reach "Finish" is the winner. For more word family practice, encourage each student to take her game home and play it with a family member.

BUILD SKILLS

This valentine activity provides hearty word family practice! Give each student a large construction paper heart that has been programmed with an -ine word. The youngster silently reads his word. On the other side of the heart, he uses a marker to write a valentine message with the word and then underlines the featured word family. The student uses provided arts-and-crafts materials to decorate the heart as desired. After each youngster reads his message aloud, display students' work below the title "Mighty Fine Valentines!"

I like you more than sunshine on a cold day!

ADD EXTENSIONS

When it comes to reinforcing the -ine word family, these books are simply divine!

Sunshine, Moonshine by Jennifer Armstrong (Random House, Inc.; 1997)

Madeline by Ludwig Bemelmans (The Viking Press, 1977)

Mr. Fine, Porcupine by Fanny Joly (Chronicle Books, 1997)

Rise and Shine!

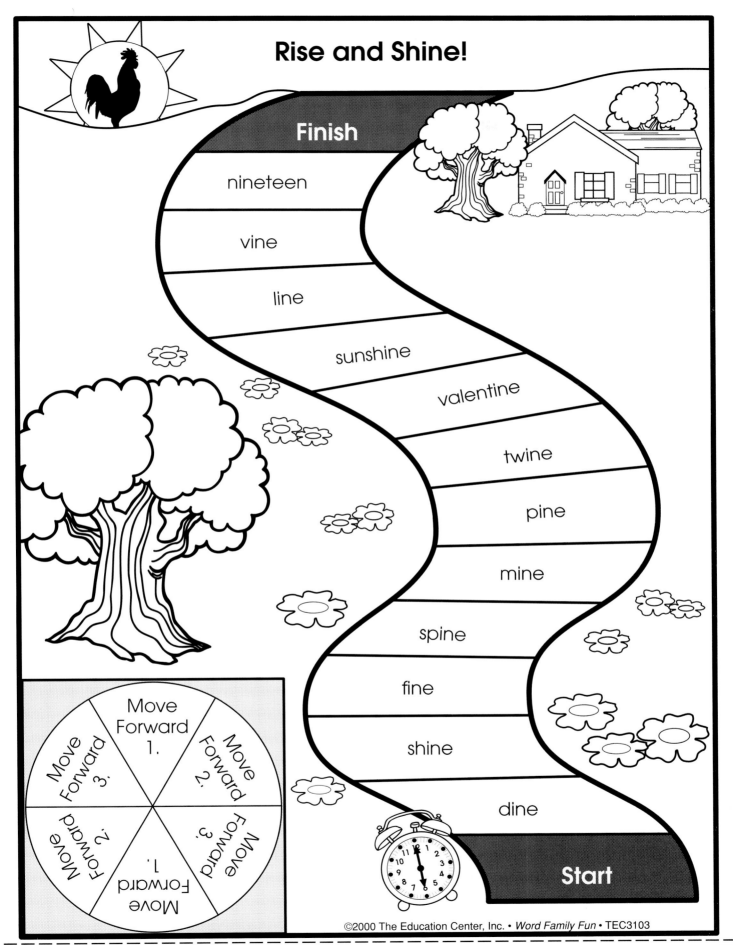

Finish

nineteen

vine

line

sunshine

valentine

twine

pine

mine

spine

fine

shine

dine

Start

Move Forward 1.
Move Forward 2.
Move Forward 3.
Move Forward 2.
Move Forward 1.
Move Forward 3.

Note to the teacher: Use with "Set the Foundation" on page 50.

-ing

bring

fling

king

ring

sing

something

spring

sting

string

swing

thing

wing

 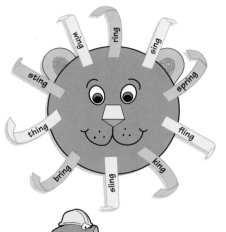

SET THE FOUNDATION

Try this idea for a royal introduction to the -ing word family! On chart paper, write the poem shown. After reading the poem aloud, lead students in a choral reading of it. With students' help, circle each -ing word in the poem. Then follow up with this "grrr-eat" word family project.

To begin, each student glues ten 1" x 5" construction paper strips to a nine-inch construction paper circle as shown. Then she uses construction paper scraps and crayons to add features so that it resembles a lion. The student uses a crayon or a marker to write a different -ing word on each strip and then slightly curls the loose end of each strip. Mount students' word-bearing lions on a board titled "A Royal Pride of -ing Words!"

The Pet for Me
I'm looking in a pet store
For the most perfect pet.
A pet with wings? A pet that sings?
Which is the pet to get?

I watch monkeys swing on ropes
And kittens play with string,
But I believe the pet for me
Is the one that's a king!

When I ask for a lion,
The clerk gives me the news—
The only place to see *that* pet
Is in the city zoo!

BUILD SKILLS

Add the crowning touch to your word family study with this class game! Give each student one copy of page 53 and 16 game markers. The youngster cuts along the dotted line and cuts the cards apart on the bold lines. Then he randomly glues the cards on the gameboard. Prepare an additional set of cards and place them in a container.

To play one round, take a card from the container and read the word aloud. Each student places a game marker on his corresponding board space. Play continues until one student has four markers in a diagonal, vertical, or horizontal row and calls "King-o!" Verify his words and then have students clear their boards for another round.

ADD EXTENSIONS

Reinforce word family skills with these titles!
Wings on Things by Marc Brown (Random House, Inc.; 1996)
Badger's Bring Something Party by Hiawyn Oram (Lothrop, Lee & Shepard Books, 1995)
Inside, Outside Christmas by Robin Spowart (Holiday House, Inc.; 1998)

Game Cards

sing	ring	king	bring
fling	sting	cling	spring
thing	string	ping	wing
ding	swing	zing	sling

Gameboard

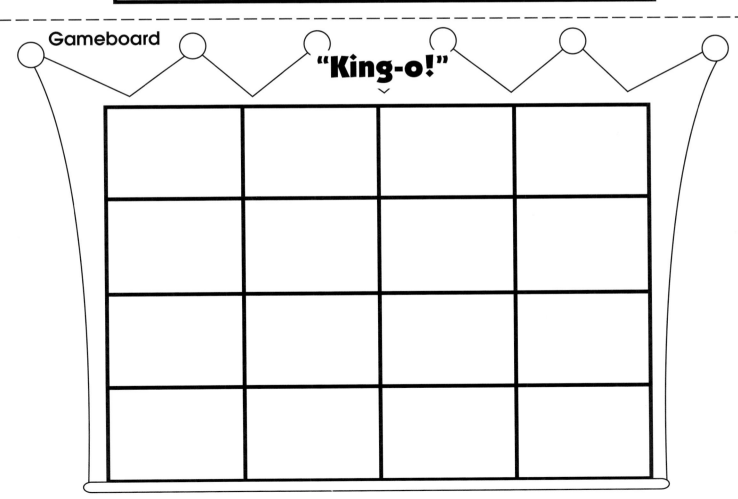

"King-o!"

-ink

blink

drink

link

mink

pink

rink

shrink

sinks

thinking

twinkle

wink

SET THE FOUNDATION

When does the night sky twinkle the most? When it's used to introduce the *-ink* word family! Write the first verse of "Twinkle, Twinkle, Little Star" on chart paper and use the directions and patterns on pages 58 and 59 to assemble a word framer. To introduce the song, share *Twinkle, Twinkle, Little Star* by Iza Trapani (Whispering Coyote Press, Inc.; 1997). Lead the class in the song; then use the word framer to isolate "twinkle" in the title. Have students read the word and find each place that it occurs in the song. Point out that "twinkle" has smaller words within it. To demonstrate, place the word framer on "twinkle," and then slide the strip and framer to isolate "wink." After students read the word, frame and read "ink." Explain that "ink" is a word *and* a word family. Review the word list on this page; then follow up with this star-studded book idea.

To make a class book, each student uses a star template to make four yellow construction paper stars. He labels each one with an *-ink* word and glues the stars on a sheet of blue construction paper. Then the youngster adds small gold adhesive stars to resemble Trapani's night sky illustrations. Bind students' completed pages into a book titled "Twinkling Word Family." Now that's a stellar reading reference!

BUILD SKILLS

Students' word family skills take wing with this fine-feathered project! Give each student one copy of the flamingo pattern and four copies of the wing pattern on page 55. The youngster labels each wing and the flamingo with an *-ink* word. She colors the patterns to make a pink flamingo and carefully cuts them out. The student hole-punches the cutouts where indicated and then uses a brad to attach the wings as shown. Each student uses the words to write a story about the flamingo on provided paper. Then she mounts her story on a slightly larger sheet of pink paper. Display each youngster's story with her flamingo below the title "In the Pink!"

ADD EXTENSIONS

Encourage students to look for the *-ink* word family in this delightful literature! *Oh, the Thinks You Can Think!* by Dr. Seuss (Random House, Inc.; 1975) *Pinky and Rex* by James Howe (Aladdin Paperbacks, 1998) *Little Pink Pig* by Pat Hutchins (Greenwillow Books, 1994)

Wing

Flamingo

-ip

chip

clip

drip

flip

hip

lip

ripping

ship

sip

skip

trip

zipper

SET THE FOUNDATION

Set sail for reading and listening fun with Nancy Shaw's *Sheep on a Ship* (Houghton Mifflin Company, 1992)! To prepare, list these words on chart paper: *drip, rip, ship, slip, tip, trip,* and *whip.* Read the book aloud one or more times for listening pleasure and then point out the *-ip* word family in the title. Display the list of words and explain that these *-ip* words are from the story. Lead students in chorally reading the words.

Next, have the class estimate how many times in all the listed *-ip* words appear in the story. As you slowly reread the book, ask each student to raise a hand each time he hears one; make a tally mark beside the word on the chart. Total the marks and compare the results with the estimate. Now that's a word family idea that you can count on!

BUILD SKILLS

Students are sure to flip over this word family booklet! Give each student a white construction paper copy of page 57. The youngster colors the pictures, cuts out the cards along the bold lines, and hole-punches the cards where indicated. Next, she stacks the letter cards atop the "sh" on the large card and attaches them with a looseleaf ring. To the left of the letter cards, she attaches the picture cards in the same manner. To use the booklet, the student flips to a picture card, flips to the letter(s) needed to form the corresponding word, and then reads the word.

ADD EXTENSIONS

Looking for a fun twist on fill-in-the-blank exercises? Try this small-group idea! Program each of several sentence strips with a sentence that has an *-ip* word, leaving a blank for the featured word. Cut a horizontal slit above the blank and slide a paper clip into the slit as shown. Write each missing *-ip* word on a separate card. If desired, also prepare one or two word cards that do not complete any of the sentences. Display the sentences and cards in random order. Read each sentence with students and invite a youngster to identify the card that completes it. Ask him to share his reasoning for choosing the card and then insert it in the paper clip. After every sentence is complete, have each youngster write and illustrate his favorite one on provided paper.

My family and I took a trip

sh **ip**

sh **ip**

ch **r** **z** **l** **cl**

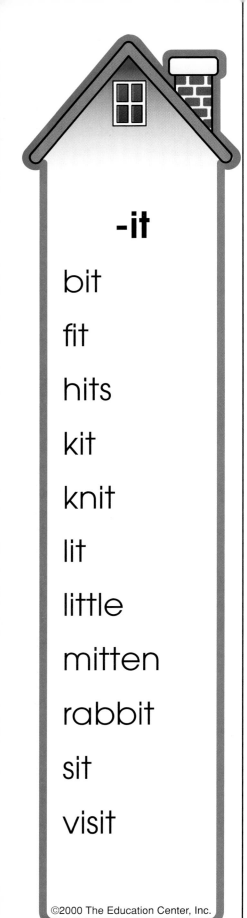

-it

bit

fit

hits

kit

knit

lit

little

mitten

rabbit

sit

visit

©2000 The Education Center, Inc.

SET THE FOUNDATION

Who better to help introduce the -it word family than the itsy bitsy spider? Before sharing a storybook version of the spider's well-known climb, prepare a word framer. To do so, cut out one tagboard copy of each pattern on page 59. Place the back atop the front and align the center openings. Tape the back in place, leaving the shorter sides open; then insert a 1³/₄" x 9" tagboard strip.

Read aloud *The Itsy Bitsy Spider* by Iza Trapani (Whispering Coyote Press, Inc.; 1997). Write the title on chart paper and use the word framer to frame *itsy*. After students identify the word, slide the strip to frame *it*, and then have students read the word family aloud. After a volunteer frames *bitsy* and its word family, list the -it words shown on this page. Invite volunteers to read and frame each word and word family in a like manner. For a "spider-ific" extension, have students recall the things the spider climbed. Ask each youngster to write and illustrate a sentence about the spider climbing a different object and then underline the -it word family each time it appears in his work.

The <u>it</u>sy b<u>it</u>sy spider climbed up the rabb<u>it</u> hutch.

BUILD SKILLS

For word family practice that's sure to be a hit, try this sorting game! Make two large masking tape squares on the floor. Place a card labeled "A Hit!" in one square to designate an area for -it words and a card labeled "Does Not Fit" in the other for words that are not in the word family. Gather a class supply of plastic lids such as the ones from margarine tubs. Use a permanent marker to program half the lids with -it words and the other half with random words.

To play, give each student one lid and divide the class into two teams of equal size. Alternating between the teams, each player, in turn, stands and reads the word on his lid aloud. He identifies the corresponding square and gently sails the lid, flying-disc-style, into it. The player earns one point if he identifies the correct square and one point if the lid lands in it. The team with the greater score wins.

ADD EXTENSIONS

For a bit of word family reinforcement, check out these titles!
The Mitten Tree by Candace Christiansen (Fulcrum Publishing, 1997)
My New Kitten by Joanna Cole (Morrow Junior Books, 1995)
Little White Duck by Walt Whippo (Little, Brown and Company; 2000)

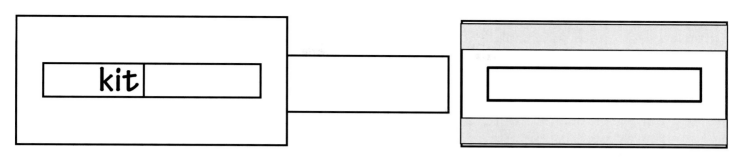

Assembled Word Framer

Back

Cut.

Front

Cut.

-ock

block

clock

dock

flock

hockey

jockey

knock

lock

rock

shock

socks

stocking

SET THE FOUNDATION

Tune in to the -ock word family with this rockin' introduction! Program ten cards with the following: bl, cl, d, fl, kn, l, -ock, r, s, and sh. Share Possum Come A-knockin' by Nancy Van Laan (Alfred A. Knopf, Inc.; 1992). Ask students what they notice about the words knock, knockin', and rockin'. Lead them to conclude that they are in the -ock word family. As you reread the book, have students listen carefully for the words knockin' and rockin'. Each time a student hears one of the words, he should knock softly on his desk (or another appropriate surface).

To follow up, display the prepared cards. Invite one child to hold up the -ock card. Say an -ock word that can be formed with this card and one other card. Ask another student to identify the card that has the needed letter(s) and have him hold it next to the -ock card to form the word. Then continue with different students and the remaining cards in a like manner.

BUILD SKILLS

It's time to make -ock words! Lead the class in reciting the nursery rhyme "Hickory, Dickory, Dock." Then give each student a copy of page 61. To assemble her clock, she colors the clock center and the outer edge of the clock face, leaving the letter spaces white. She cuts out both pieces and cuts out the triangle on the hour hand (provide assistance as necessary). The youngster uses a brad to fasten the two circles together as shown.

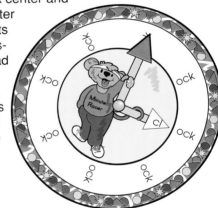

To use her clock, the student turns the clock face to reveal a letter or a blend and then reads the resulting word. After each child has read all of the words, challenge her to create a two-line rhyme using two of them.

ADD EXTENSIONS

Tickle youngsters' funny bones with a knock-knock sentence break! In advance, write a different sentence with an -ock word on each of several sentence strips. Use a sticky note to cover the -ock word in each sentence. Post one sentence and invite a student to join you in saying the following:

Student: "Knock-knock"
Teacher: "Who's there?"
Student: "-Ock."
Teacher: "-Ock who?"

The student answers by guessing the word that is hidden by the sticky note. If the child guesses correctly, reveal the word. If the answer is incorrect, repeat the process with another student. Continue the activity until the -ock word in each sentence has been uncovered.

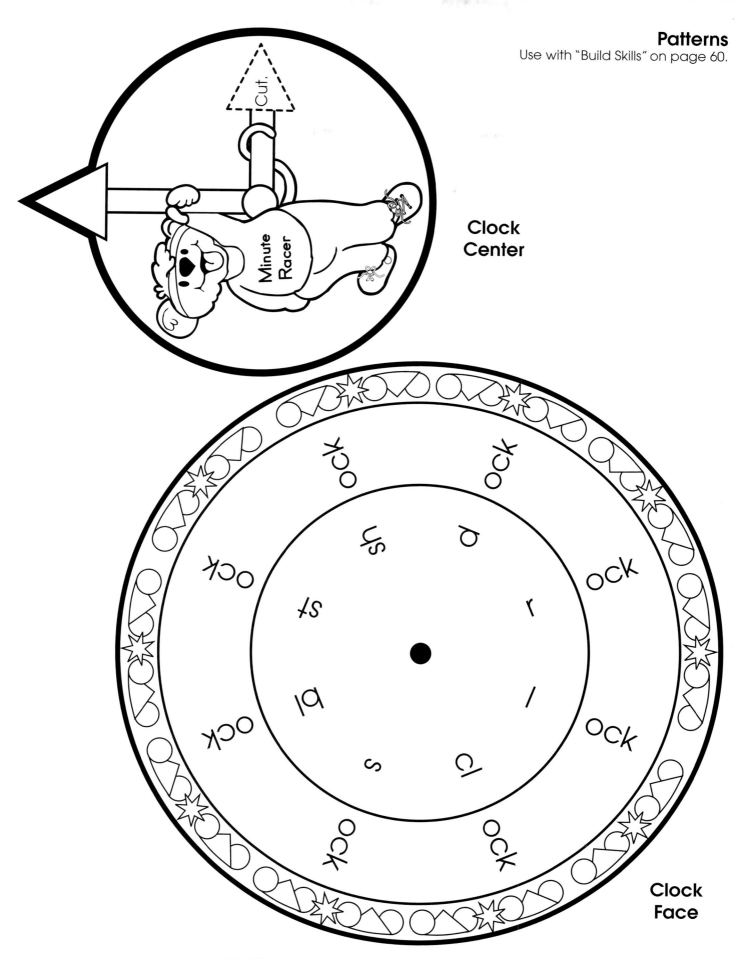

Clock
Center

Clock
Face

-oke

awoke

broke

choke

joke

poke

smoke

spoke

woke

yoke

SET THE FOUNDATION

Here's an activity that's sure to have students thinking (and reading) on their feet! Share *The Hokey Pokey* by Sheila Hamanaka (Simon & Schuster Books for Young Readers, 1997). Point out that two words in the title have *-oke* in them. After students identify them, brainstorm additional *-oke* words. Then use some of the brainstormed words in a special version of "The Hokey Pokey."

To prepare, announce an *-oke* word. Each student writes the word on a paper strip. With the help of a nearby classmate, he tapes it around his right wrist, keeping the word visible. He uses dictated words to prepare strips for his left wrist and each of his ankles and then tapes them in place as directed. Modify the lyrics of "The Hokey Pokey" to create a verse for each *-oke* word (see the example), and invite students to make the corresponding actions.

You put your [joke wrist] in,
You put your [joke wrist] out,
You put your [joke wrist] in
And you shake it all about!

BUILD SKILLS

Keep *-oke* word skills rolling right along! Show students a picture of a bicycle. Explain that the name for one part of the bicycle is an *-oke* word. After students conclude that the word is *spoke,* point out the spokes in the picture. Announce that each student will make a word wheel that has different-colored spokes.

To prepare, list six colors on the board. Each student cuts out a copy of the pattern on page 63 and uses a brad to attach it to an eight-inch construction paper circle. She reads each letter or blend on a spoke and circles the one that completes the *-oke* word below. She fills in the blank(s) and then colors the spoke a listed color. The youngster completes the rest of her paper, using each color only once and turning the wheel as necessary for easy reading. Then announce each color, in turn, and have each student read her corresponding word to a partner.

ADD EXTENSIONS

Tickle students' funny bones with mystery *-oke* words! On the board, write five or more sentences, each with an *-oke* word represented by a blank. Nearby, draw four blanks to secretly represent the word *joke.* Explain that for each sentence students complete and read aloud as a class, you will randomly fill one of the blanks with a letter to spell a mystery reward. After students complete four sentences, have a volunteer identify the completed word *(joke);* then share your favorite joke book.

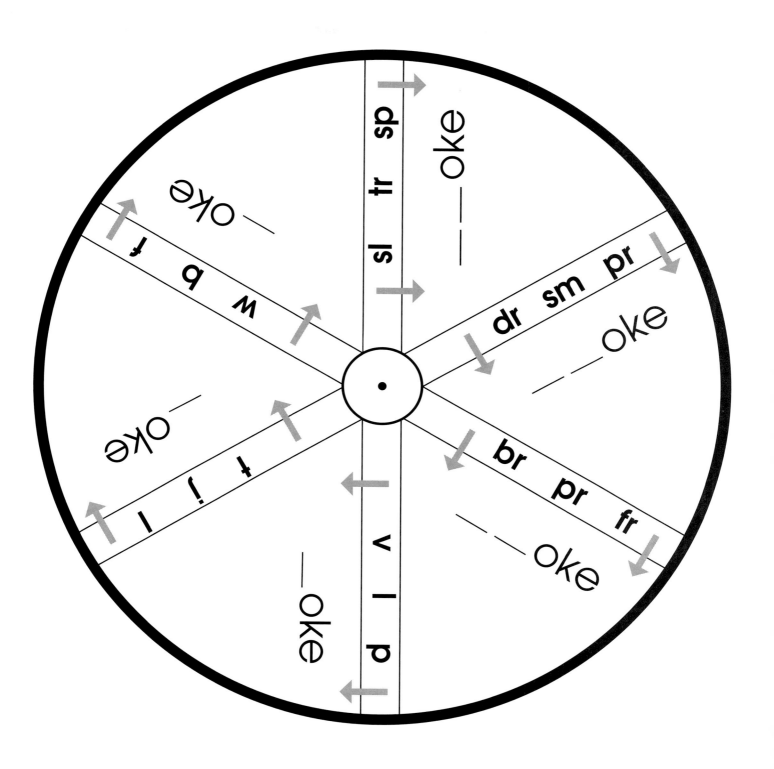

-op

chop

crop

drop

flop

gumdrop

hopping

mop

pop

popcorn

shop

stop

top

SET THE FOUNDATION

This word family introduction is the tops! Write the poem shown on chart paper. Make a separate word card for each -op word every time it occurs in the poem. Display the poem and then point to each word as you read the poem with students. After rereading it, use highlighting tape (available from Crystal Springs Books, 1-800-321-0401) or a bright marker to mark the -op word family in the title. Have students find the -op words in the poem and mark them in a similar manner.

Next, distribute the cards. As the class chorally reads the poem, ask each cardholder to raise his card every time he hears his word. Redistribute the cards and then reread the poem in a like manner. Continue until every youngster has had a turn as a cardholder.

Pop the Bubbles!

Blowing great big bubbles
Down at the bus stop.
Watching the wind take them
Up to the treetops.

Seeing great big bubbles
Now starting to drop.
Hearing all the bubbles
Going "Pop! Pop! Pop!"

BUILD SKILLS

Here's an idea that's sure to keep reading skills popping! Give each student eight white construction paper copies of the whole popcorn patterns and one copy of each popcorn half on page 65. Instruct her to cut out the patterns on the bold lines and glue each half onto a different piece of popcorn to form an -op word.

Next, give each student a white paper lunch bag. The youngster uses a red crayon to decorate the bag to resemble a vendor's popcorn bag. Then she places her popcorn inside. Pair students. Each partner, in turn, takes a piece of popcorn from her bag. She reads the word aloud (with help from her partner as necessary) and then sets the popcorn aside. Play continues until the partners have read all of their words. For a tasty finale, serve freshly popped popcorn. Mmm!

ADD EXTENSIONS

When it comes to reinforcing the -op word family, these books are the cream of the crop!

Mop Top by Don Freeman (Puffin Books, 1978)

The Hippo Hop by Christine Loomis (Houghton Mifflin Company, 1995)

Hippity Hop, Frog on Top by Natasha Wing (Simon & Schuster Books for Young Readers,1994)

Use with "Build Skills" on page 64.

Whole Popcorn

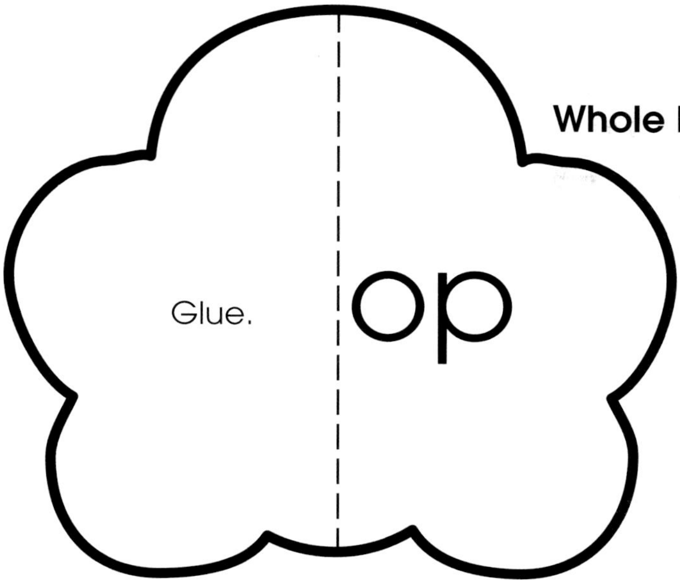

Glue.
op

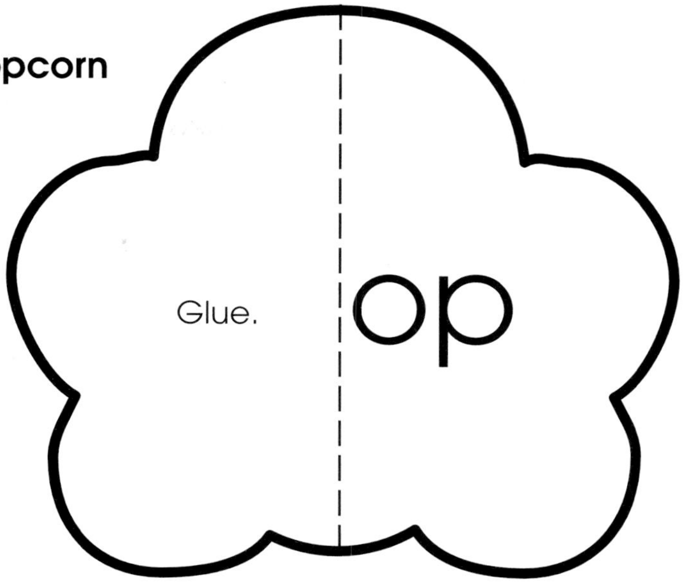

Glue.
op

Popcorn Halves

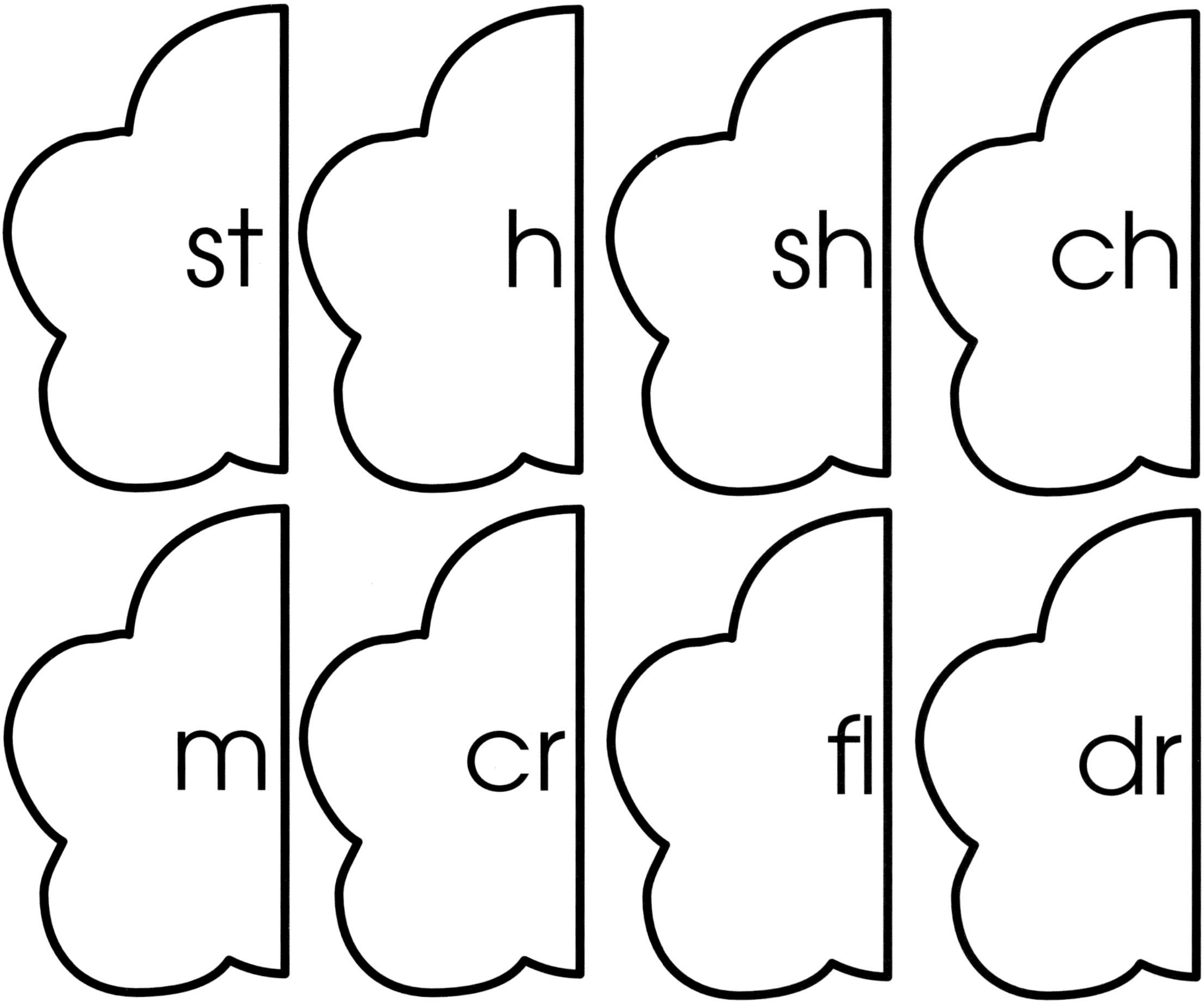

st
h
sh
ch
m
cr
fl
dr

-ore

chore

core

lore

more

pore

score

shore

snore

store

tore

wore

SET THE FOUNDATION

Here's a fitting introduction to the *-ore* word family! Read *Mary Wore Her Red Dress, and Henry Wore His Green Sneakers* by Merle Peek (Clarion Books, 1988) aloud. Write "wore" on the board and underline the word family. Write a student-generated list of *-ore* words on the board; then have each youngster create her own colorful lineup of *-ore* words.

To begin, give each student one copy of page 67 and a 20-inch length of yarn. The youngster labels each pattern with an *-ore* word, colors it, and cuts it out. She lays the yarn horizontally on her desk to represent a clothesline. Then the student folds the tabs of each cutout over the yarn, glues them in place, and ties each end of the yarn to make a loop. Each youngster reads her words aloud and then uses her name and a chosen cutout in a verse like the one shown.

Helen wore a yellow dress, yellow dress, yellow dress,
Helen wore a yellow dress and it said "shore!"

BUILD SKILLS

This oral language activity provides word family practice galore! Recite the poem below and then ask a volunteer to supply the missing word. After verifying his response, invite the student to think of a different word, use the rhyme to describe it, and challenge his classmates to guess it. Continue in a like manner for a desired number of turns.

I'm thinking of a word
That ends with *-ore*.
It starts with [initial consonant, blend, or digraph],
So the word must be _____.

ADD EXTENSIONS

This interactive *-ore* display makes a lot of "cents"! Cut the corners from one short side of each of 12 index cards and hole-punch the card between the cuts. Program one side of each card with an *-ore* word and the other side with a price. Thread a length of yarn through each resulting price tag, tie the ends, and hang the tag with its price showing on a board titled "Welcome to the -ore Word Store!"

To use the display, call out a price. Ask a student to find the corresponding tag, turn it over, and read the word aloud. After the youngster turns the tag back over, continue in a like manner for a desired amount of time. To vary the activity, display a set of play coins. Have students count the coins to find the correct price tag and then read it aloud.

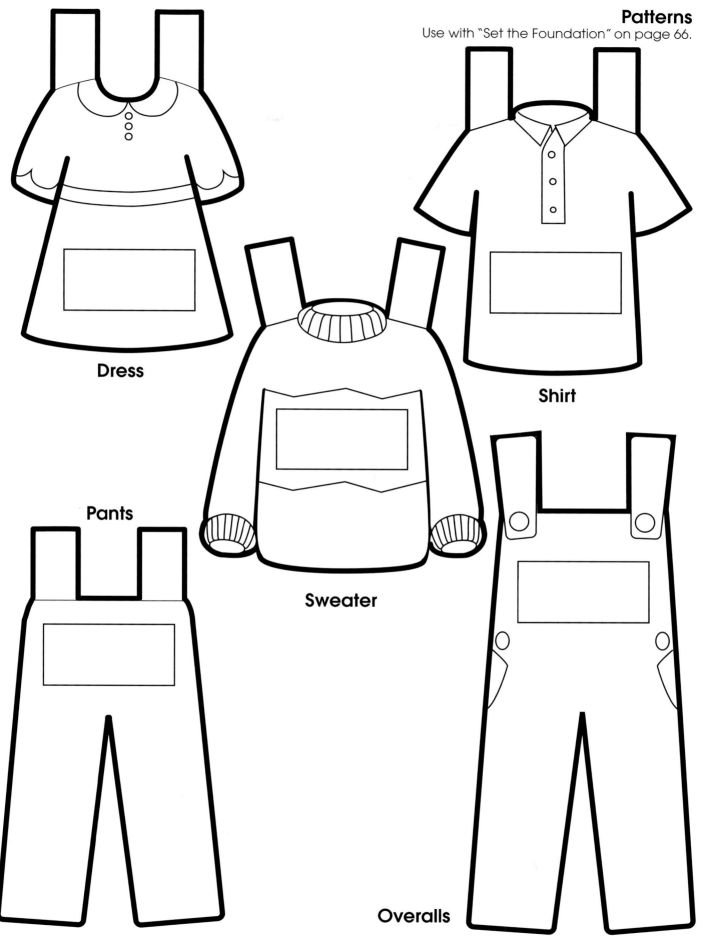

Dress

Shirt

Pants

Sweater

Overalls

-ot

cot

dot

forgot

got

hot

knot

lot

not

pot

shot

slot

spot

SET THE FOUNDATION

Help students spot -ot words with this creative idea! Share *McSpot's Hidden Spots: A Puppyhood Secret* by Laura L. Seeley (Peachtree Publishers Ltd., 1997), a rhyming tale about a self-proclaimed "spot king." After pointing out the -ot words in the title, have students brainstorm other words in this word family. Then invite youngsters to create a word-filled display of fanciful spotted critters.

To begin, remind students that when it comes to picturing animals with spots, McSpot's imagination knows no bounds. The worried dalmatian imagines spotted critters of every shape, size, and species. Give each student a sheet of drawing paper and several large, round self-adhesive labels. Have the youngster picture an animal that does not usually have spots and then draw the animal on the provided paper. To transform his animal into a one-of-a-kind spotted critter, the student writes a different -ot word on each label and then adheres it to his animal. For a royal finishing touch, he adds a construction paper crown cutout. Display students' completed work below the title "Who's the Real Spot King?"

BUILD SKILLS

Students bone up on the ABCs of word families with this reproducible activity! In advance, prepare one tagboard bone cutout for each of the following words: *cot, dot, forgot, hot, pot, shot,* and *slot.* Attach a piece of magnetic tape to the back of each bone, and display the bones on a magnetic chalkboard (or use loops of tape to adhere the bones to a board). After reviewing the words, have students work as a class to put them in alphabetical order. For individual alphabetizing practice, have each student complete a copy of page 69.

ADD EXTENSIONS

When it comes to reinforcing word family skills, this lively activity hits the spot! To prepare, program a number of tagboard circles with -ot words. Place the circles on the floor in a desired arrangement and use two-sided tape to secure the circles in place. Each student, in turn, stands a designated distance from the circles. He tosses a beanbag toward them, reads the word on which the beanbag lands or to which it is closest, and uses the word in an original sentence. Play continues until each student has taken one turn. What a fun way to develop a class of hotshot readers!

Name _____

-ot

Hot on the Trail With Spot

Begin at the star.

Connect the dots in ABC order.

What does Spot find at the end of the rainbow?

Use the picture to answer the riddle.
(*Hint:* The answer is an **-ot** word.)

A ___ ___ ___ of bones!

Bonus Box: On the back of this sheet, write a story about the day that Spot forgot where he hid his bones. Draw a picture for your story.

• cot

• dot

• forgot

• got

• hot

slot

shot •

• knot

pot •

not •

lot •

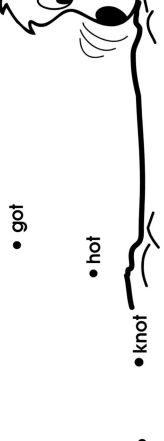

©2000 The Education Center, Inc. • *Word Family Fun* • TEC3103 • Key p. 95

Note to the teacher: Use with "Build Skills" on page 68.

-uck

bucket

buckle

Chuck

cluck

duck

luck

puck

stuck

trucker

tuck

SET THE FOUNDATION

This word family introduction is just ducky! In advance, use the patterns on page 71 to make a number of mother duck and duckling tracers. Read *One Duck Stuck* by Phyllis Root (Candlewick Press, 1998) aloud. Then write on the board the following words from the story: *duck, stuck, luck, muck,* and *spluck*. Lead students in chorally reading the words; then point out the *-uck* word family in each one. As you reread the book, have each student give the thumbs-up sign every time he hears a listed word. For a fine-feathered follow-up, each student uses the tracers to make one mother duck and six ducklings from yellow construction paper. He cuts a 12" x 18" sheet of blue construction paper in half lengthwise, then glues the two resulting strips together to make one long strip.

Next, pair students. Give each student one copy of the word cards (page 71). Each partner cuts his cards apart and stacks them. In turn, each partner takes a card from his stack, reads it aloud, and writes the word on his mother duck. Then he glues the duck on one end of his strip. In a like manner, each partner labels and glues his ducklings in a line behind his mother duck. He uses crayons to add details as desired and then reads his completed lineup to his partner.

BUILD SKILLS

Set students on the road to reading and writing fun with these colorful trucks! Post a list of *-uck* words on the board. Give each student a 9" x 12" sheet of light-colored construction paper. The youngster places it lengthwise on her desk to represent the trailer of a semitrailer truck. She writes on the paper an original sentence that has at least one word from the *-uck* word family. Then she underlines the *-uck* word(s). To complete her truck, the youngster uses crayons, construction paper scraps, and glue to add a cab, wheels, and other desired details. Post the completed trucks below the title "Trucking Right Along With Word Families!" If desired, invite youngsters to add construction paper road signs and traffic lights to the display.

I always <u>buckle</u> up when I ride in my friend's <u>truck</u>.

ADD EXTENSIONS

Count on plenty of chuckles with these entertaining titles!
Duck in the Truck by Jez Alborough (HarperCollins Publishers, Inc., 2000)
Isaac the Ice Cream Truck by Scott Santoro (Henry Holt and Company, 1999)
"Yuck" from *Falling Up: Poems and Drawings by Shel Silverstein* by Shel Silverstein (HarperCollins Children's Books, 1996)

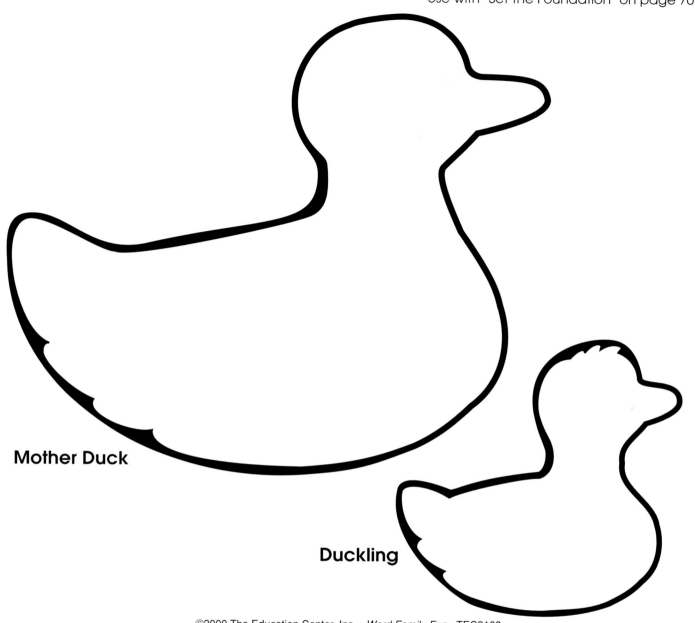

Mother Duck

Duckling

©2000 The Education Center, Inc. • Word Family Fun • TEC3103

Word Cards

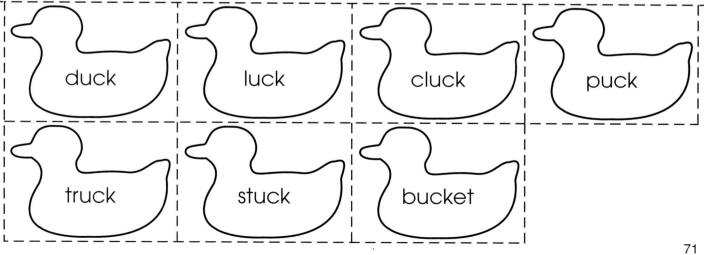

duck

luck

cluck

puck

truck

stuck

bucket

-ug

bugs

hug

jug

juggle

ladybug

mug

plug

slug

snug

tug

SET THE FOUNDATION

Start your -ug word family study with these eye-catching critters! Begin by reading *Bugs! Bugs! Bugs!* by Bob Barner (Chronicle Books, 1999). Write *bug* on a sheet of chart paper and underline the -ug word family. As students brainstorm other -ug words, add them to the chart. Ask students to underline the word family in each word. Then have each youngster use the words with this colorful bug project.

To begin, give each student a copy of the circle pattern on page 73. She uses the pattern to make six construction paper circles. In the center of each of five circles, she writes a different -ug word. The youngster slightly overlaps the circles and carefully glues them together to make a long, colorful bug as shown. She uses construction paper scraps and crayons to add details such as facial features and legs. Display students' creative creepy-crawlies below the title "Going Buggy Over the -ug Word Family!"

BUILD SKILLS

Serve up mugfuls of word family practice with these nifty booklets! To make a booklet, each student colors a white construction paper copy of the booklet cover (page 73) and signs his name. The youngster cuts out the cover and places it atop four 5$\frac{1}{2}$" x 8$\frac{1}{2}$" pieces of white paper and one 6" x 9" piece of construction paper. He staples the entire stack where indicated and then cuts the paper to the shape of the mug. To complete his booklet, the student lists -ug words on the first page. On each remaining page, he uses a different word from his list in a sentence and illustrates his work. If desired, serve hot chocolate in disposable mugs as each youngster reads his booklet to an assigned partner.

ADD EXTENSIONS

Reinforce word skills *and* put empty milk jugs to good use with this unique center idea. Gather a number of clean, empty plastic milk jugs and cut away the top of each one. Divide students into small groups and give each group a permanent marker and a prepared jug. Have each group brainstorm -ug words and write them on its jug. After verifying students' work, collect the jugs, put a set of letter manipulatives in each jug, and place the jugs in a center. When a student visits the center, she pours the letters out of one jug and then uses them to spell the listed words.

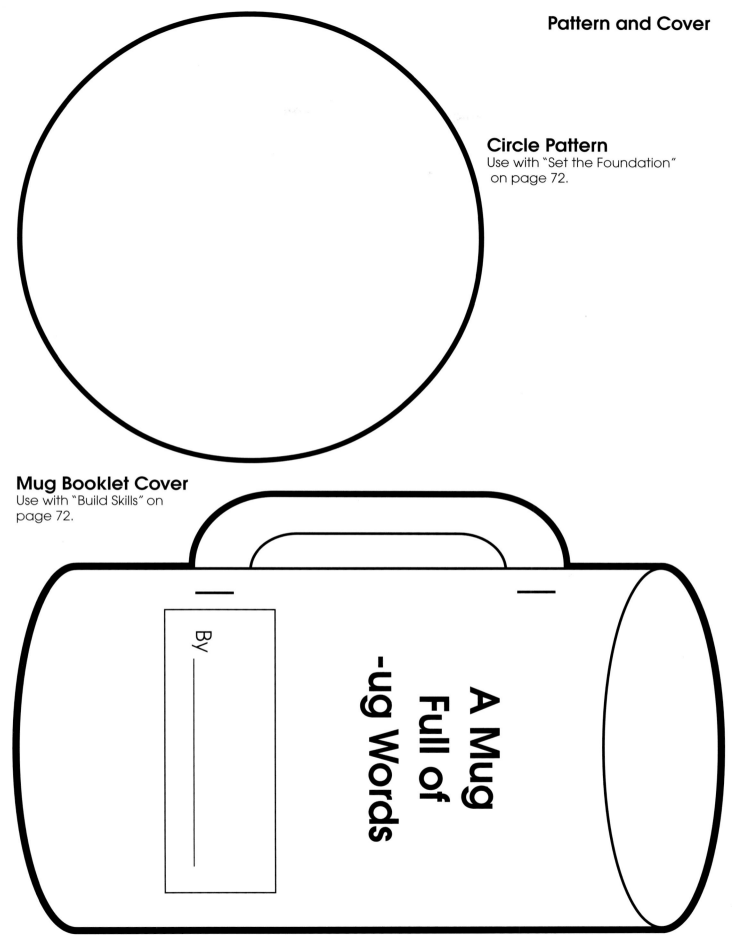

Circle Pattern
Use with "Set the Foundation"
on page 72.

Mug Booklet Cover
Use with "Build Skills" on
page 72.

By _____

A Mug
Full of
-ug Words

-ump

bump

clump

dump

jump

lump

plump

pump

pumpkin

stump

thump

SET THE FOUNDATION

Jump-start your -ump word family study with this "eggs-traordinary" idea! To prepare, cover the top half of a bulletin board with white paper and the bottom half with gray paper. Use a marker to draw bricks on the bottom half so that it resembles a wall. Share *Little Lumpty* by Miko Imai (Candlewick Press, 1996). Ask students what the words *Lumpty, Dumpty,* and *jump* have in common. Lead them to conclude that they are in the -ump word family. Explain that students will use the word family to design a new wall for the fictional town of Dumpty.

To do so, have students brainstorm -ump words. Write each word in a brick on the board. Give each student a copy of page 75 (enlarge the patterns, if desired). The young-ster colors and cuts out the character and a chosen accessory; then he glues them together. Add students' characters and the title "Dumpty's -ump Word Wall" to complete this "eggs-cellent" word reference.

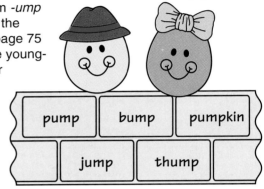

BUILD SKILLS

All the king's horses and all the king's men couldn't put one well-known egg back together, but your students are sure to have more success with these word-filled eggs! Program a number of paper strips with sentences that include -ump words. Cut between the words to divide each sentence into a desired number of pieces. Number the back of each piece for self-checking and place the pieces inside a plastic egg. Tuck the eggs in a basket filled with cellophane grass. Place the basket in a center.

After reading *Little Lumpty* (see the above idea), arrange for each student to visit the center. The youngster removes and sequences the sentence pieces from each egg and then turns them over to check her work.

ADD EXTENSIONS

Give students a new perspective on lumps and bumps with Judith Thurman's cleverly written poem titled "Lumps." Copy the poem from *The Random House Book of Poetry for Children* selected by Jack Prelutsky (Random House, Inc.; 1983) onto a sheet of chart paper. Read the poem aloud one or more times for listening pleasure; then have students underline every -ump word. Next, reread the poem with students, reading only the words that do not belong in the featured word family and having the class read only the -ump words. What a fun way to team up word family practice and poetry!

-unk

bunk

chipmunk

chunk

dunk

flunk

junk

junkyard

plunk

shrunk

skunk

sunk

trunk

SET THE FOUNDATION

Word family skills are sure to blossom with this unique garden! Share *Junk Pile!* by Lady Borton (Philomel Books, 1997), a story about an imaginative girl who sees beauty in a junkyard. Then have students make a flowery display modeled after the hubcap flowers in the story. To begin, write a student-generated list of *-unk* words on the board. Divide students into groups of six. Give each group six small paper plates, six nine-inch aluminum foil squares, and one six-inch construction paper circle.

To make a flower, ask each group to write *-unk* words on its circle. Have each student wrap a foil square over the front of a plate. Help each group mount its circle and plates on a bulletin board and add a construction paper stem and leaves as shown. Then title the display "Words Help Our Junkyard Garden Grow!"

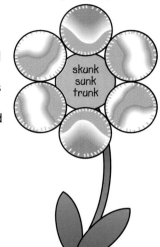

skunk
sunk
trunk

BUILD SKILLS

These chipmunks are hungry for *-unk* words! To make a word game, each student needs a paper lunch bag and a copy of page 77. She initials the back of each card for easy sorting and colors the chipmunk. The youngster cuts out the cards and chipmunk, glues the chipmunk on the bag, and then cuts through the bag along the dotted line (provide assistance as needed).

To play, pair students and have partners combine their cards. One player shuffles the cards and stacks them facedown. Each player stands her bag upright and folds over the top. Alternating turns, each player draws a card and reads it aloud. If it is an *-unk* word, she "feeds" it to her chipmunk by dropping it into the bag through the mouth opening. If it is not, she places it in a discard pile. The game continues until all of the cards have been drawn. The player with the most cards wins.

ADD EXTENSIONS

This small-group idea is packed with word family practice! Have each group use arts-and-crafts materials to decorate a shoebox so that it resembles a trunk. Give each group several *-unk* word cards and have the youngsters put them in the box. In each group, one student removes a card and orally uses the word to begin a story. Each remaining group member, in turn, continues the story in a like manner. After every word card has been used, one group member concludes the story. If desired, place the word-filled trunks in a center for individuals or partners to write their own treasured tales.

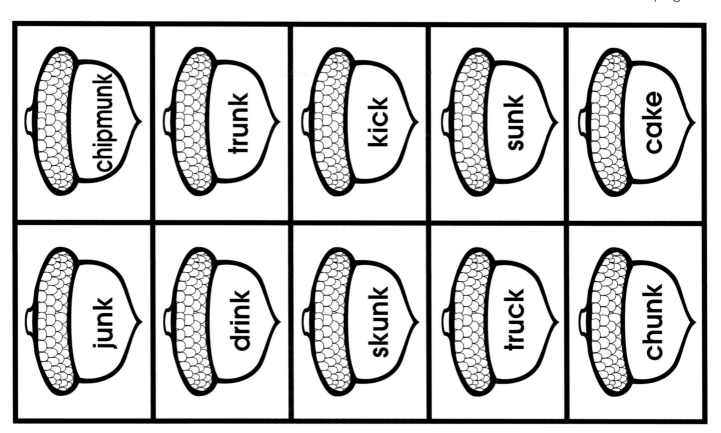

chipmunk | trunk | kick | sunk | cake

junk | drink | skunk | truck | chunk

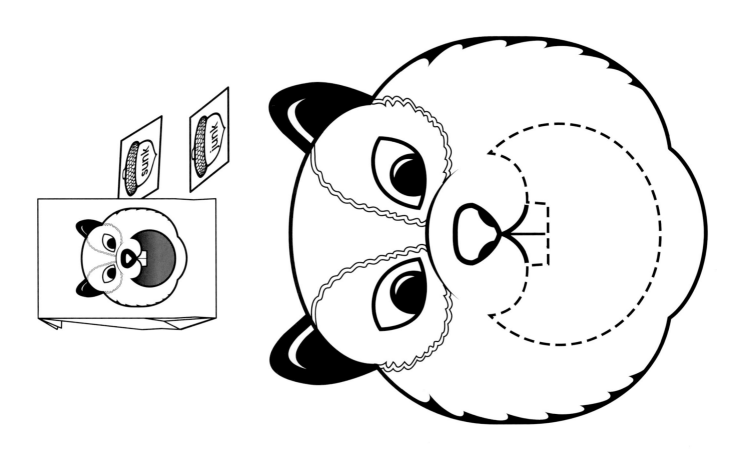

FOR ANY WORD FAMILY

Count on this assessment tool and these quick-as-a-wink activities to be valuable additions to your teacher's toolbox of reading ideas!

SKILLS SURVEY

ASSESSMENT

Develop a blueprint for reading success with this informal assessment tool! Make a tagboard copy of page 92. Cut along the bold lines to make three cards. Laminate the cards for durability, if desired. Copy page 93 to make a class supply of student forms.

To assess one student's ability to decode words with common word families, show him the prepared copy of List 1. Use index cards to frame one word at a time. As the youngster reads the words, make a check mark on a student form beside each one that he reads correctly. If he reads a word incorrectly, write what he said (the miscue) beside it. If the youngster makes no response for a word, write "NR." Continue with List 2 if the student reads the majority of List 1 with ease. Follow up with List 3, if appropriate.

Next, study the results for any notable strengths or weaknesses. Record these at the bottom of the sheet. Use selected word family activities to provide needed skill reinforcement. Periodically use the assessment tool as appropriate to reassess the youngster's skills and to record his progress.

SOUNDS LIKE FUN!

PHONEMIC MANIPULATION

Students are sure to be all ears with this phonemic awareness activity! Announce a word from a chosen word family and have students chorally repeat it. Using the format shown, ask them to make a substitution for the initial letter and then say the resulting word. Continue with a desired number of words. For an added challenge, use words that have initial blends or digraphs.

> Say "back."
>
> Say it again with /t/ instead of /b/.

MYSTERY MESSAGE

CLOZE

Deliver daily word family practice with a morning mystery message! In advance, write a message to the class on a sheet of chart paper, using blanks in place of letters for selected word families (see the illustration). Lead students in reading the message. Have volunteers fill in the missing letters and identify the corresponding word families. If desired, collect an entire month of messages, then sequence and bind them between covers to make a unique class diary.

September 17

Good morning!
Today we w i l l go
to the library after we eat
our sn a c k s.

Your friend,
Miss Bartlett

SPELLING SAVVY

BUILDING WORDS

Here's a letter-perfect word family idea for the entire class! Give each student an individual chalkboard, a stick of chalk, and a scrap of felt for an eraser. Prepare an overhead projector and obtain a set of magnetic letters. Select one or more word families to reinforce. With the projector turned off, have a volunteer use the letters to spell a dictated word on it as each of the other youngsters writes the word on her chalkboard. Then ask the volunteer to turn the projector on and each of the other youngsters to hold up her board to show her word. Verify the correct spelling. Continue with other volunteers and words for a desired period of time. What a nifty way to quickly see how each of your young spellers is progressing!

SENSATIONAL SORTING

SORTING AND CLASSIFICATION

Energize word family practice with this versatile sorting activity! Obtain a number of large blank cards that is equal to the number of students in half your class. Choose three or more word families. Program each card with a word from one of the families, being sure to make at least two cards for each family. Shuffle the cards and distribute them. Have each student who is holding a card read it aloud. Then ask him to stand at the front of the room and hold the card so that it is visible to his classmates. Challenge the seated students to tell the card-holding youngsters how to group themselves so that they are sorted by word family. After the students are grouped, have a representative from each group announce its word family and each group member read his word aloud. Collect the cards, distribute them to the seated youngsters, and have students trade roles for more word family practice.

ROLL A RIME!

NAMING WORDS WITH RIMES

It's no toss-up! This class activity is a surefire winner! Cover a square box with paper. Program each side with a different word family (rime). Seat students in a circle on the floor. Gently toss the cube, read the word family on the top side, and then name a word that has it. Pass the cube to the student on your left. Have her take a turn in a similar manner, asking her classmates for suggestions if she is unable to name a word that has not been named before. Continue around the circle until every student has taken one turn.

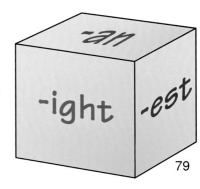

Busy Word Builders

The busy builders need your help!
Cut apart the letter cards.
Use the cards to make **-ack**, **-ap**, and **-at** words on your desk.
Then write each word below its family.

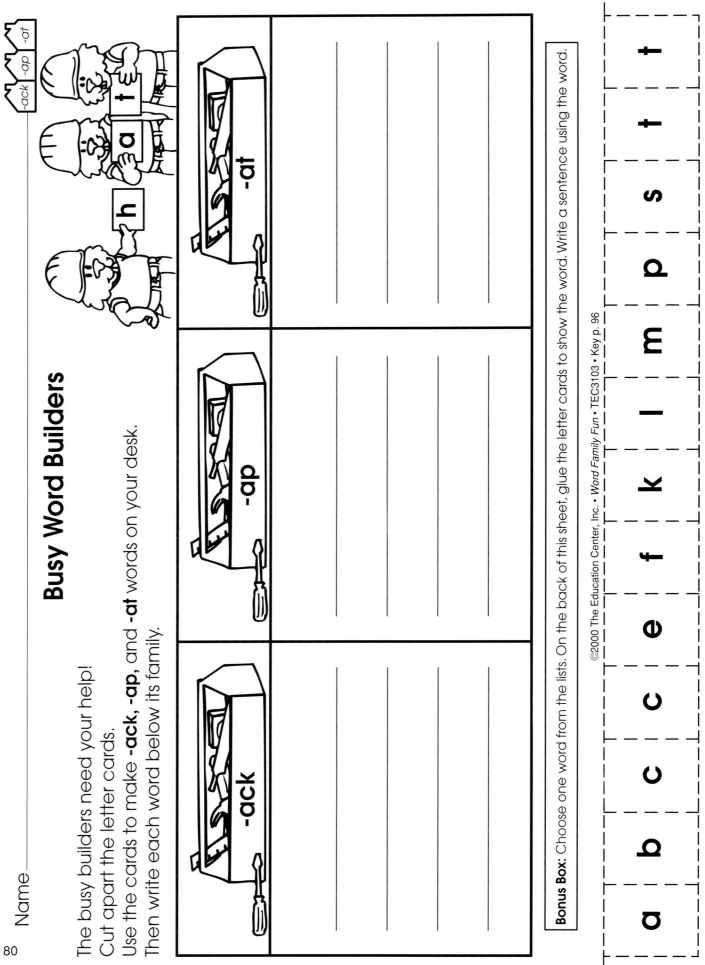

-ack | -ap | -at

Bonus Box: Choose one word from the lists. On the back of this sheet, glue the letter cards to show the word. Write a sentence using the word.

| a | b | c | c | e | f | k | l | m | p | s | t | t |

Name _____

On the Right Track

Color and **cut** out each train car.
Say the name of each picture.
Glue it on the track that has the same word family.

1. -ail

2. -ake

3. -an

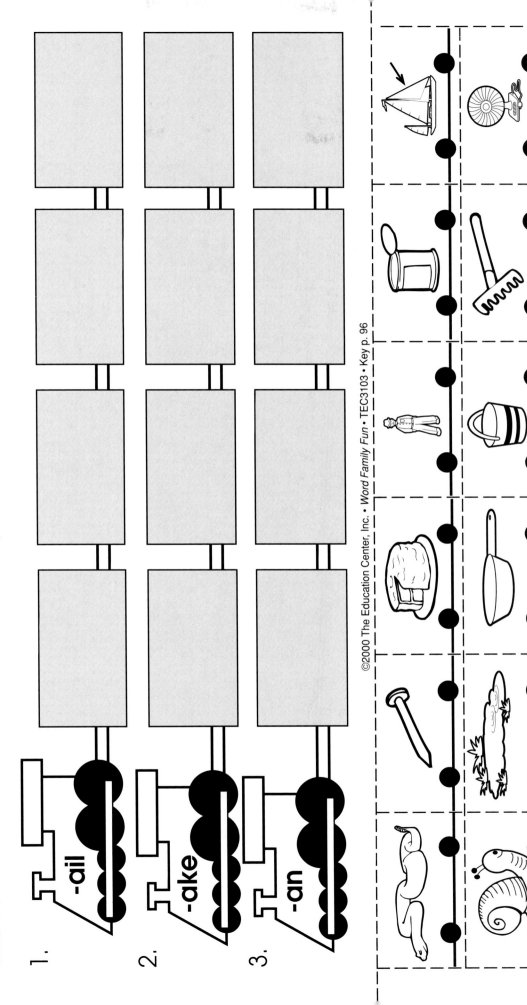

Name _____

-eat -ell -est

Under the Sea

Write **-eat, -ell,** or **-est** to complete each word.
Use the color code to color the shells.

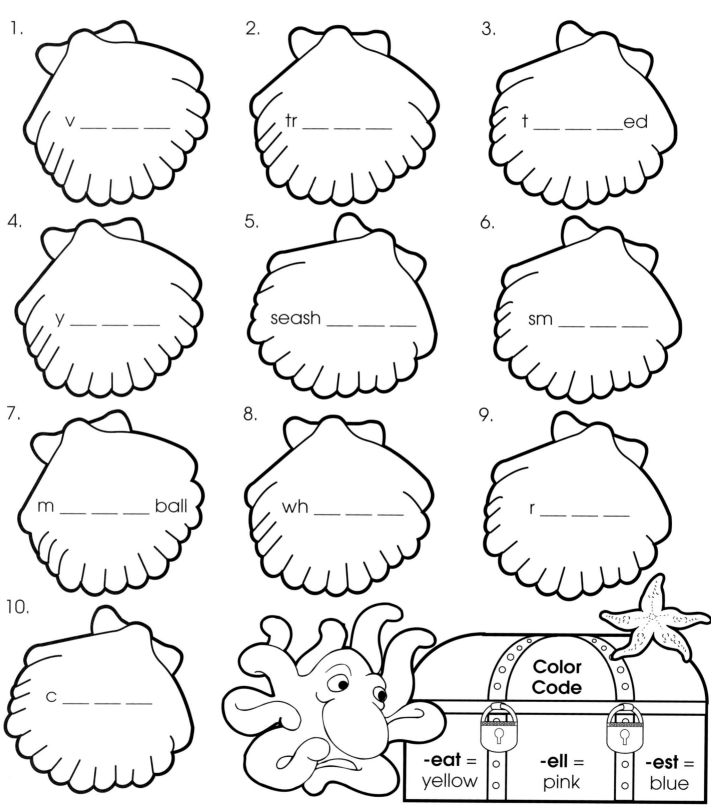

1. v _ _ _ _

2. tr _ _ _ _

3. t _ _ _ _ ed

4. y _ _ _ _

5. seash _ _ _ _

6. sm _ _ _ _

7. m _ _ _ _ ball

8. wh _ _ _ _

9. r _ _ _ _

10. c _ _ _ _

Color Code

-eat = yellow   -ell = pink   -est = blue

82   ©2000 The Education Center, Inc. • *Word Family Fun* • TEC3103 • Key p. 96

Names _____

-eat -ell -est

Tic-Tac-Toad

Directions for Two Players

1. Cut apart the cards. Stack them facedown.

2. In turn, draw a card.

3. If you can make a word, say it. Put the card on the gameboard.

4. If you cannot make a word, place the card at the bottom of the stack.

5. The first player to cover three squares in a row wins.

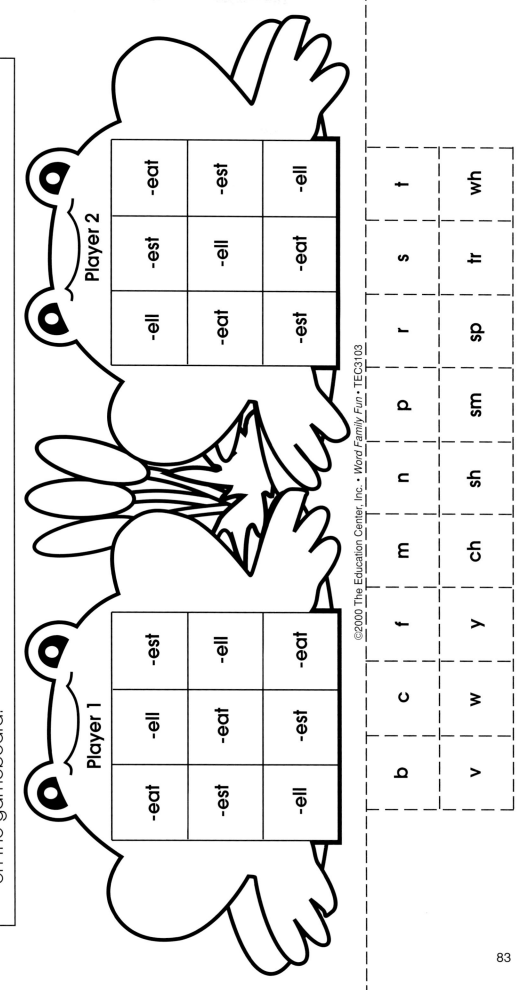

Player 2

-eat	-est	-ell
-est	-ell	-eat
-ell	-eat	-est

Player 1

-est	-ell	-eat
-ell	-eat	-est
-eat	-est	-ell

©2000 The Education Center, Inc. • Word Family Fun • TEC3103

b	c	f	m	n	p	r	s	t
v	w	y	ch	sh	sm	sp	tr	wh

Word Wings

Follow your teacher's directions.

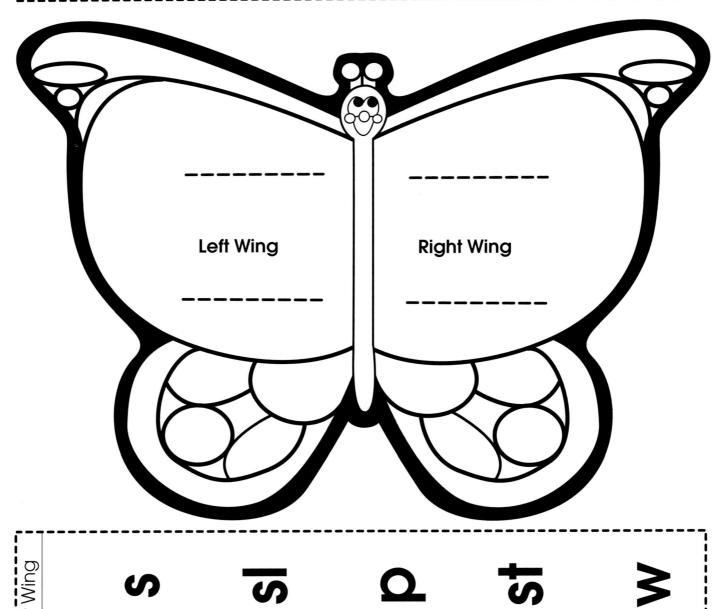

Right Wing

ing ink ick

Left Wing

Right Wing

Left Wing

s sl p st w

Note to the teacher: Give each student a copy of this page. The student colors the butterfly pattern. Then he cuts out all the patterns and cuts along the dotted lines on the wings (provide assistance as necessary). The youngster inserts each strip into the correct wing. He slides the strips to make as many words as he can and writes the words on provided paper.

Fun at the Sock Hop

Write your name on the sock.
Write an **-ock** or **-op** word for
   each picture.
Color and cut out the patterns.
Hole-punch each circle.
Use a brad to attach the foot
   to the back of the sock.

Finished Sample

Silly Sock Hop

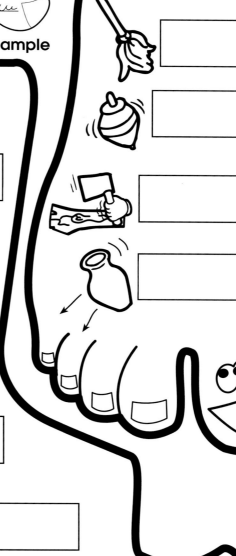

Name

Name _____

Words to Cheer About

Use each letter, blend, or digraph to make a different word.
Then cross it out.

br	ch	ch	m	n	sc	sl	t	t	tr	w	w

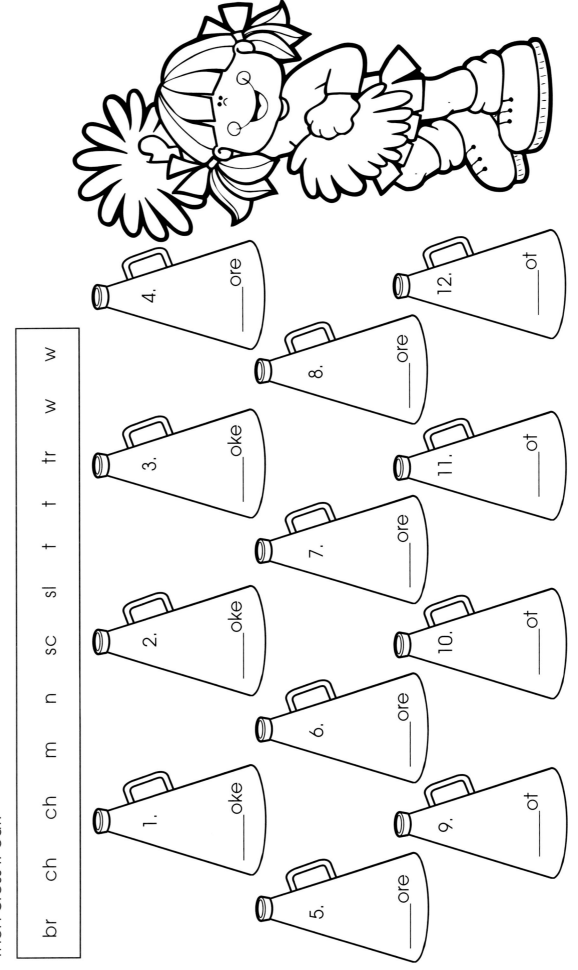

1. ____oke
2. ____oke
3. ____oke
4. ____ore
5. ____ore
6. ____ore
7. ____ore
8. ____ore
9. ____ot
10. ____ot
11. ____ot
12. ____ot

-oke   -ore   -ot

Name _____

Wormy Words

Read the name of each worm.
Read the Word Bank.
Write each word on the correct apple.

-uck -ump -unk

Word Bank

bumper	cluck
chunky	pump
duckling	skunk
dump	stuck
flunk	stump
jumping	truck
junk	trunk
tuck	

Punky

Grumpy

Lucky

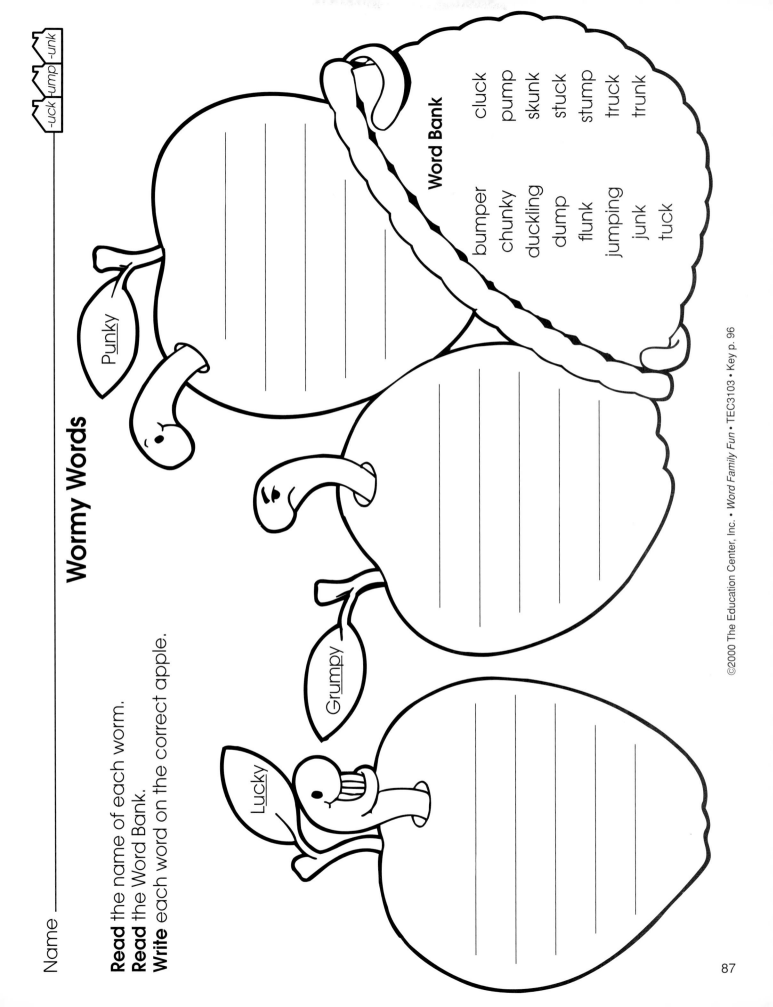

©2000 The Education Center, Inc. • *Word Family Fun* • TEC3103 • Key p. 96

Name _____

Up, Up, and Away!

Follow your teacher's directions.

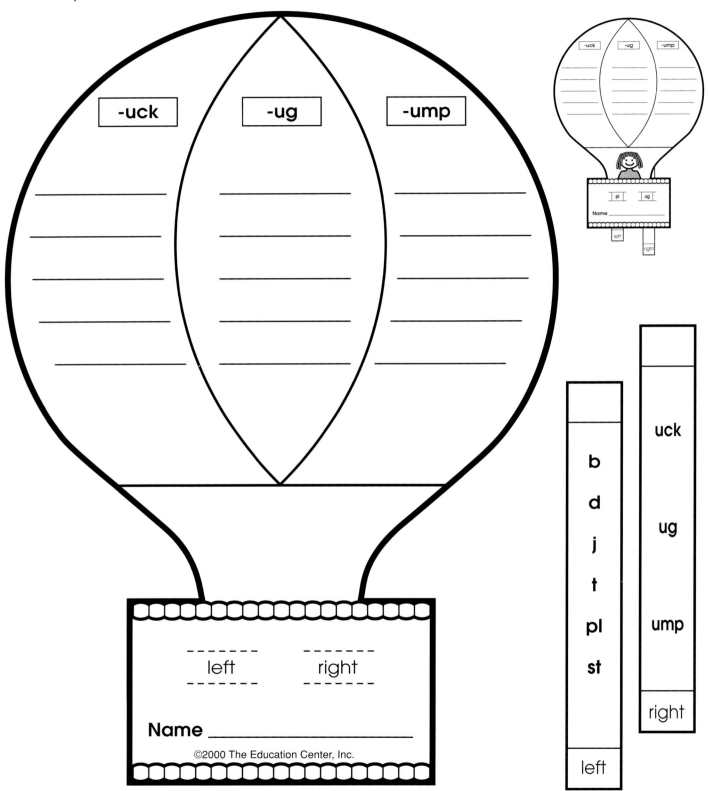

-uck   -ug   -ump

left   right

Name _____

©2000 The Education Center, Inc.

uck

ug

ump

right

b
d
j
t
pl
st

left

©2000 The Education Center, Inc. • Word Family Fun • TEC3103 • Key p. 96

Note to the teacher: Give each student a copy of this sheet. She cuts out the balloon and letter strips and then cuts on the dotted lines (provide assistance as needed). The student inserts the strips into the slits. She slides the strips to make a word and then writes the word in the correct section on the balloon. The youngster continues until she has written a word on every line. Then she draws a picture of herself in the balloon.

88

Bone Mix-Up

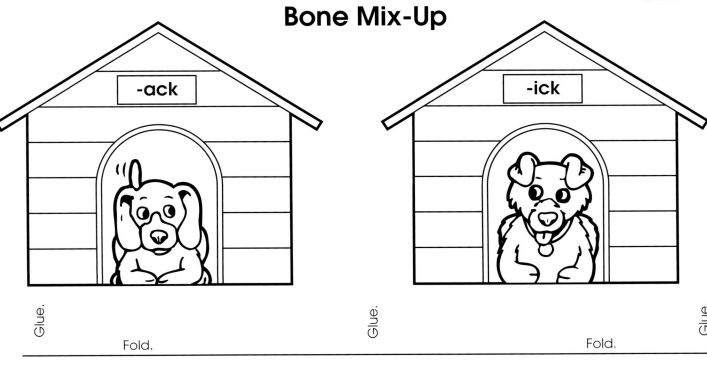

-ack

-ick

Glue.   Fold.   Glue.   Fold.   Glue.

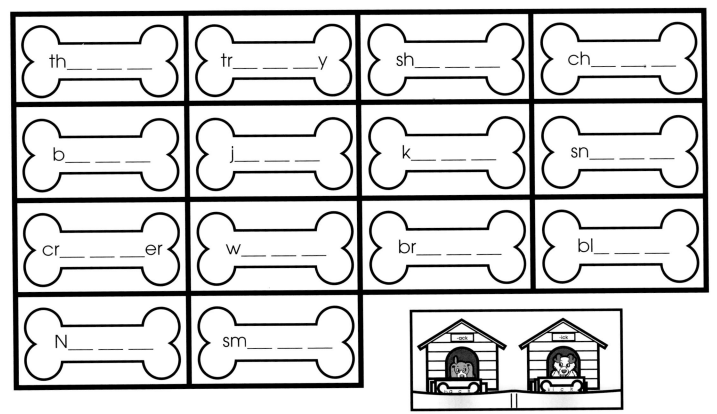

th____   tr____y   sh____   ch____

b____   j____   k____   sn____

cr____er   w____   br____   bl____

N____   sm____

Note to the teacher: Give each student a copy of this sheet. The student completes each word using *-ack* or *-ick*. She cuts out the cards on the bold lines. She cuts along the dotted line and then folds and glues the doghouse pattern where indicated to make two pockets. The youngster reads each card and puts it in the correct pocket.

-ice -ide -in

Smooth Sailing

Cut out the word family boats.
For each sail, **find** the boat that can complete
  all of its words.
Glue the boat.
Write the words.

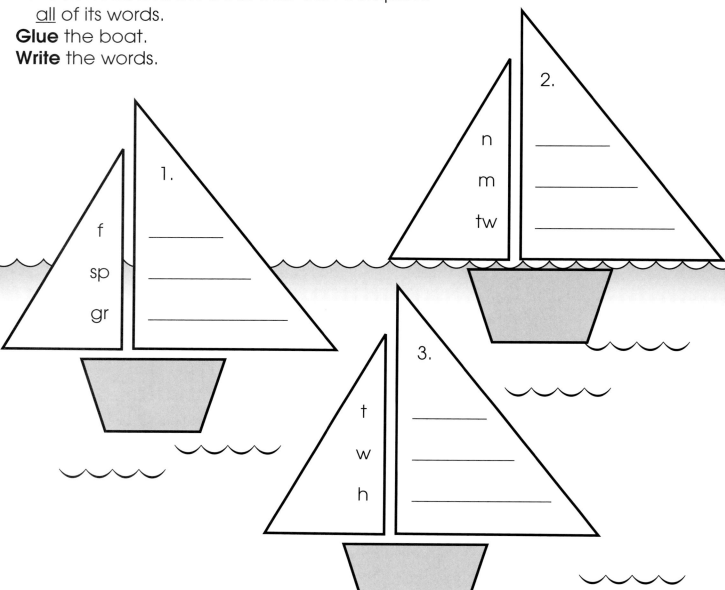

Bonus Box: On the back of this sheet, write two more words from the **-in** word family. Draw a picture for each one.

©2000 The Education Center, Inc. • *Word Family Fun* • TEC3103 • Key p. 96

- -

Word Family Boats

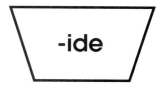

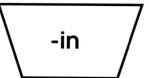

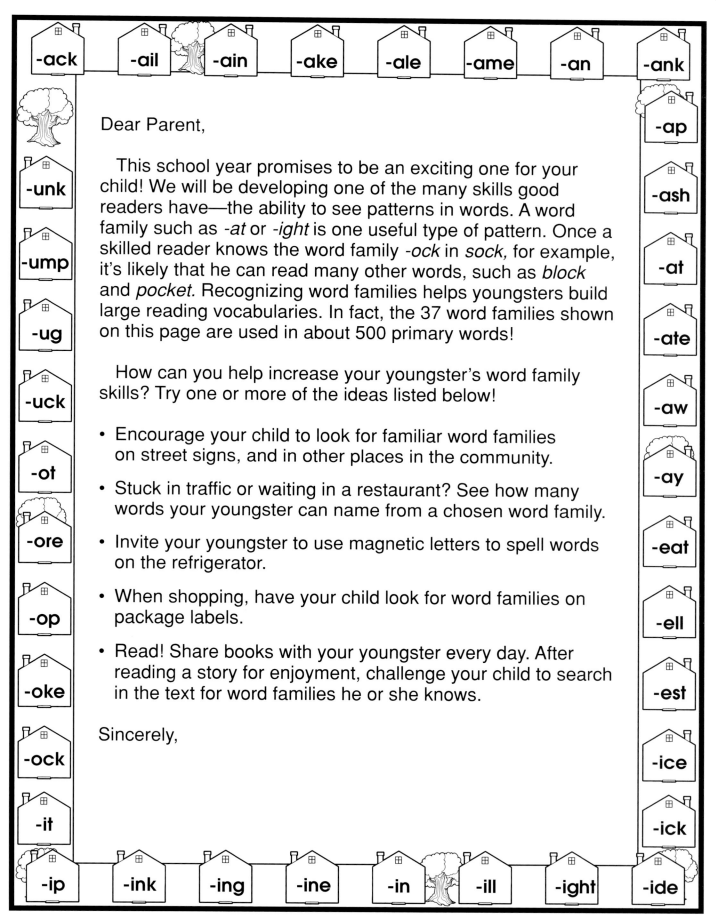

-ack · -ail · -ain · -ake · -ale · -ame · -an · -ank · -ap · -ash · -at · -ate · -aw · -ay · -eat · -ell · -est · -ice · -ick

-unk · -ump · -ug · -uck · -ot · -ore · -op · -oke · -ock · -it

-ip · -ink · -ing · -ine · -in · -ill · -ight · -ide

Dear Parent,

This school year promises to be an exciting one for your child! We will be developing one of the many skills good readers have—the ability to see patterns in words. A word family such as *-at* or *-ight* is one useful type of pattern. Once a skilled reader knows the word family *-ock* in *sock,* for example, it's likely that he can read many other words, such as *block* and *pocket.* Recognizing word families helps youngsters build large reading vocabularies. In fact, the 37 word families shown on this page are used in about 500 primary words!

How can you help increase your youngster's word family skills? Try one or more of the ideas listed below!

• Encourage your child to look for familiar word families on street signs, and in other places in the community.

• Stuck in traffic or waiting in a restaurant? See how many words your youngster can name from a chosen word family.

• Invite your youngster to use magnetic letters to spell words on the refrigerator.

• When shopping, have your child look for word families on package labels.

• Read! Share books with your youngster every day. After reading a story for enjoyment, challenge your child to search in the text for word families he or she knows.

Sincerely,

Note to the teacher: Duplicate and then sign this page or use it as a model to write a personalized parent letter. Prepare a class supply of copies and have each student take a copy home.

91

List 1

1. back
2. pail
3. rain
4. make
5. sale
6. game
7. fan
8. bank
9. lap
10. cash
11. hat
12. gate
13. jaw
14. day
15. neat
16. bell
17. vest
18. mice
19. pick

20. wide
21. fight
22. hill
23. tin
24. nine
25. ring
26. wink
27. zip
28. kit
29. sock
30. joke
31. pop
32. more
33. hot
34. duck
35. rug
36. bump
37. junk

List 2

1. stack
2. snail
3. train
4. brake
5. stale
6. flame
7. plan
8. thank
9. trap
10. crash
11. that
12. skate
13. straw
14. tray
15. wheat
16. shell
17. chest
18. twice
19. thick

20. bride
21. flight
22. still
23. chin
24. shine
25. sting
26. think
27. drip
28. skit
29. clock
30. smoke
31. flop
32. chore
33. spot
34. truck
35. slug
36. plump
37. chunk

List 3

1. inside
2. mitten
3. sunshine
4. flashlight
5. pancake
6. mailbox
7. blinks
8. uphill
9. priced
10. lately
11. trucker
12. stocking
13. pumpkin
14. matter
15. seesaw
16. resting
17. meatball
18. raindrop
19. thankful

20. seashell
21. haystack
22. nickname
23. drugstore
24. snapshot
25. chipmunk
26. salesman

Note to the teacher: Use with "Skills Survey" on page 78.

Name _____ Date _____

Student Form

List 1	List 2	List 3
1. back _____	1. stack _____	1. inside _____
2. pail _____	2. snail _____	2. mitten _____
3. rain _____	3. train _____	3. sunshine _____
4. make _____	4. brake _____	4. flashlight _____
5. sale _____	5. stale _____	5. pancake _____
6. game _____	6. flame _____	6. mailbox _____
7. fan _____	7. plan _____	7. blinks _____
8. bank _____	8. thank _____	8. uphill _____
9. lap _____	9. trap _____	9. priced _____
10. cash _____	10. crash _____	10. lately _____
11. hat _____	11. that _____	11. trucker _____
12. gate _____	12. skate _____	12. stocking _____
13. jaw _____	13. straw _____	13. pumpkin _____
14. day _____	14. tray _____	14. matter _____
15. neat _____	15. wheat _____	15. seesaw _____
16. bell _____	16. shell _____	16. resting _____
17. vest _____	17. chest _____	17. meatball _____
18. mice _____	18. twice _____	18. raindrop _____
19. pick _____	19. thick _____	19. thankful _____
20. wide _____	20. bride _____	20. seashell _____
21. fight _____	21. flight _____	21. haystack _____
22. hill _____	22. still _____	22. nickname _____
23. tin _____	23. chin _____	23. drugstore _____
24. nine _____	24. shine _____	24. snapshot _____
25. ring _____	25. sting _____	25. chipmunk _____
26. wink _____	26. think _____	26. salesman _____
27. zip _____	27. drip _____	
28. kit _____	28. skit _____	
29. sock _____	29. clock _____	
30. joke _____	30. smoke _____	
31. pop _____	31. flop _____	
32. more _____	32. chore _____	
33. hot _____	33. spot _____	
34. duck _____	34. truck _____	
35. rug _____	35. slug _____	
36. bump _____	36. plump _____	
37. junk _____	37. chunk _____	

Comments

_____

_____

_____

_____

_____

_____

Note to the teacher: Use with "Skills Survey" on page 78.

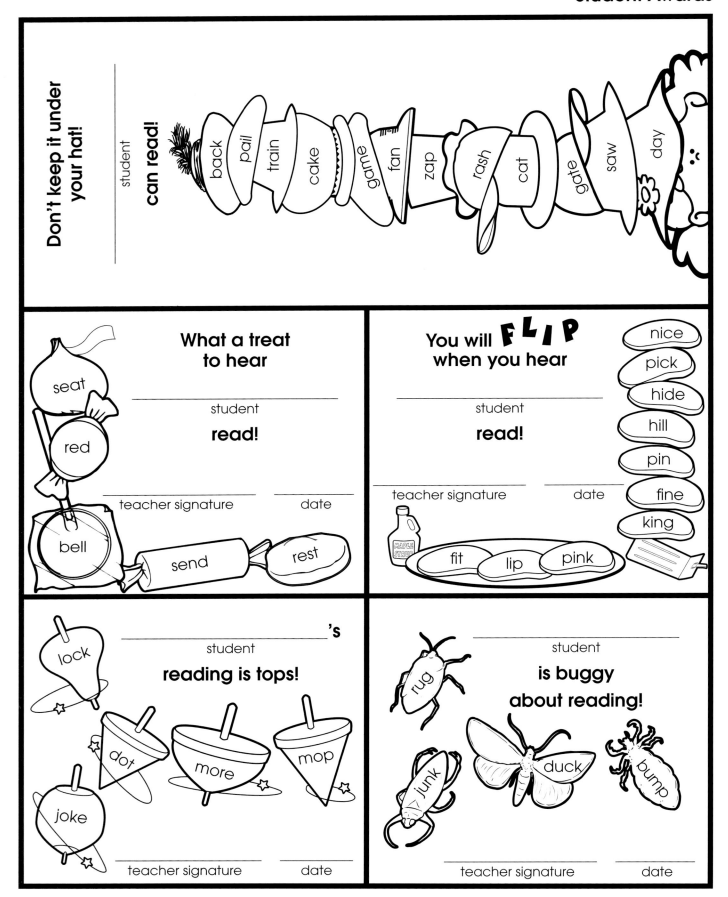

Don't keep it under your hat!

_____ student

can read!

back
pail
train
cake
game
fan
zap
rash
cat
gate
saw
day

What a treat to hear

seat

red

bell

_____
student

read!

_____ _____
teacher signature   date

send   rest

You will FLIP when you hear

_____
student

read!

_____ _____
teacher signature   date

nice
pick
hide
hill
pin
fine
king

fit   lip   pink

_____'s
student

reading is tops!

lock

dot

more

mop

joke

_____ _____
teacher signature   date

_____
student

is buggy about reading!

rug

junk   duck   bump

_____ _____
teacher signature   date

Note to the teacher: Copy the student awards and distribute them as desired to recognize youngsters' reading achievements.

Answer Keys

Page 7
These words should be written on the back of each student's mailbox: *pail, sail, tail, snail, trail, hail, mail, railing, fail, mailbox.*

Page 15
1. n<u>ame</u>
2. fr<u>ame</u>
3. s<u>ame</u>
4. fl<u>ame</u>s
5. t<u>ame</u>
6. g<u>ame</u>

Bonus Box: Illustrations will vary. Accept any reasonable drawing.

Page 23
1. mash
2. rash
3. cash
4. dash
5. smash
6. trash
7. flash
8. crash
9. splash

Sentences will vary but each should include a word from above.

Page 27
1. state
2. skate
3. Kate
4. gate
5. late
6. locate

Bonus Box: Illustrations will vary. Accept any reasonable drawing.

Page 47
The order of the answers on the caterpillars may vary slightly (*drill* and *still* may be on either the second or fourth caterpillar).

> I saw ten caterpillars crawling up a __hill__.
>
> They were not moving fast, but they did not stand __still__.
>
> Seeing the parade of bugs was really a __thrill__.
>
> It looked just like a caterpillar fire __drill__!

Page 63
Students should have written the following words: *poke, joke, woke, spoke, smoke, broke.*

Page 69

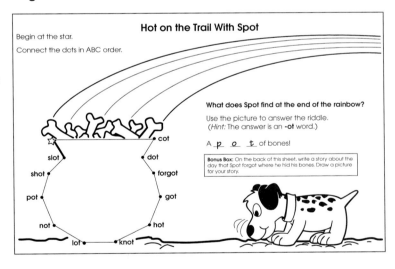

95

Answer Keys

Page 80
Possible answers include
-ack: back, backs, black, flack, pack, packet, packs, sack, smack, stack, tack, tacks
-ap: cap, caps, clap, flap, flaps, lap, laps, map, maps, sap, slap, tap, taps
-at: bat, bats, cat, cats, fat, flat, mat, mats, pat, pats, sat, stat

Page 81
The order of the cars may vary.

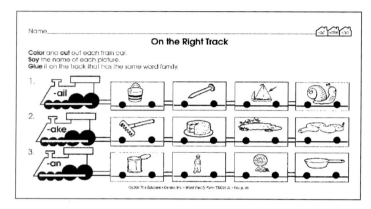

Page 82
1. vest (blue)
2. treat (yellow)
3. tested (blue)
4. yell (pink)
5. seashell (pink)
6. smell (pink)
7. meatball (yellow)
8. wheat (yellow)
9. rest (blue)
10. cell (pink)

Page 85
Sock
rocks
block
clock
rocket
pocket

Foot
mop
top
chop
drop

Page 86
The order of answers may vary slightly.
1. choke
2. broke
3. woke
4. score
5. wore
6. more
7. chore
8. tore
9. tot
10. slot
11. trot
12. not

Page 87
The order of answers may vary.
Lucky
cluck
duckling
stuck
truck
tuck

Grumpy
bumper
pump
dump
stump
jumping

Punky
chunky
skunk
flunk
junk
trunk

Page 88
The order of answers may vary.
-uck
buck
duck
tuck
pluck
stuck

-ug
bug
dug
jug
tug
plug

-ump
bump
dump
jump
plump
stump

Page 89

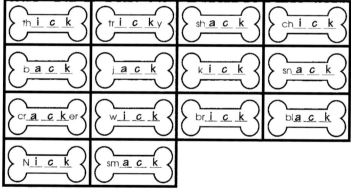

Page 90
1. fin, spin, grin
2. nice, mice, twice
3. tide, wide, hide

Bonus Box: Answers will vary. Accept any reasonable responses.